Aristophanes (c455-385BC) is the oldest comedy writer in Western literature and still one of the funniest. He wrote some forty plays, of which eleven survive. A unique blend of slapstick, fantasy, lyricism, bawdy and political and social satire, they give an unparalleled glimpse of the ancient Greeks at their most exuberant and most unbuttoned.

These lively and 'dazzlingly funny' translations by Kenneth McLeish are complemented by historically illuminating introductions by the translator and the series editor, J Michael Walton.

This is a companion volume to *Aristophanes Plays: Two*, which contains *Wasps*, *Clouds*, *Birds*, *Festival Time (Thesmophoriazousai)* and *Frogs*. A forthcoming volume, *Aristophanes & Menander*, will include *Women in Power* and *Wealth*.

Aristophanes was born in Athens about the middle of the fifth century BC. His first play was performed in 427 but produced, perhaps because of his youth, under the name of Kallistratos. The first surviving play is *Acharnians*, one of nine that represent all we have of what has come to be known as Old Comedy. All of these nine were written against the backdrop of the Peloponnesian War in which Sparta finally defeated Athens in 404BC. Two last plays from the fourth century show a change in mood and emphasis to a more social drama and are therefore to be published separately along with two plays of Menander. Aristophanes probably died in 385BC.

ARISTOPHANES

Plays: One
introduced by J Michael Walton

Acharnians
Knights
Peace
Lysistrata

*translated and introduced by
Kenneth McLeish*

series editor: J Michael Walton

METHUEN WORLD CLASSICS

These translations first published in Great Britain 1993
by Methuen Drama
an imprint of Reed Consumer Books Ltd
Michelin House, 81 Fulham Road, London SW3 6RB
and Auckland, Melbourne, Singapore and Toronto
and distributed in the United States of America by Heinemann,
a division of Reed Publishing (USA) Inc., 361 Hanover Street,
Portsmouth, New Hampshire NH 03801 3959

Reprinted 1993

An earlier version of this translation of *Knights* was published
by Cambridge University Press in 1979.

ISBN 0-413-66900-9

A CIP catalogue record for this book
is available at the British Library

Typeset by Saxon Printing Ltd, Derby in Baskerville, 10/11.
Printed and bound in Great Britain
by Cox & Wyman Ltd, Reading, Berkshire

The painting on the front cover is *Bodegón al claro de luna* by
Salvador Dalí. Transparency from Centro de Arte Reina Sofia,
Madrid, Spain. Copyright © Demarte Pro Arte BV/DACS 1993.

CONTENTS

A Note on the Translator and Series Editor

KENNETH McLEISH'S books include *The Theatre of Aristophanes*, *Shakespeare's People A-Z* and *The Good Reading Guide*. His original films and plays include *Just Do It*, *Tony* and *Vice at the Vicarage* (for Frankie Howerd). His translations include plays by all the extant Greek and Roman dramatists, and by Ibsen, Feydeau, Labiche and Goldoni. His translation of Sophocles' *Electra* was directed by Deborah Warner at the RSC in 1989; his version of Ibsen's *Peer Gynt* was directed by Declan Donnellan at the Royal National Theatre in 1990; his adaptation of Feydeau's *Pig in a Poke* was toured by the Oxford Stage Company in 1992.

J MICHAEL WALTON worked in the professional theatre as an actor and director before joining the University of Hull, where he is Head of the Drama Department. He has published three books on Greek theatre, *Greek Theatre Practice*, *The Greek Sense of Theatre: Tragedy Reviewed*, and *Living Greek Theatre: A Handbook of Classical Performance and Modern Production*. He has also published in a number of areas of more modern British and European theatre, is the editor of *Craig on Theatre* and General Editor of Methuen Classical Drama in Translation.

EDITOR'S INTRODUCTION

In the introduction to his own first volume of Collected Plays Arthur Miller records that the most radical play he ever saw was not *Waiting for Lefty*, Clifford Odets' celebrated left-wing rallying cry to 1930s America, but Jean Giraudoux's *The Madwoman of Chaillot*. *La Folle de Chaillot* was first performed in 1945. Far from being the anti-fascist polemic that its date and Miller's reaction might suggest, it is a fantasy-comedy set in a Paris which is threatened by the discovery of oil under Chaillot. The 'free people', whose representative is a Ragpicker, appeal for help to Countess Aurelia, the 'Madwoman' of the title. The pimps, he tells her, have taken over the world, 'their eyes empty, their expression not human'.

Dismayed, the Madwoman decides it is time for action if she is to prevent Paris being dug up to satisfy the Prospectors and the Company Presidents. She invites them all to visit her cellar, sends them down a trapdoor, led by their noses towards the smell of oil, and bolts it after them. 'Well, there we are,' she announces. 'The world is saved. And you see how simple it all was? Nothing is ever so wrong in this world that a sensible woman can't set it right in the course of an afternoon.' Hers is a solution which might well have appealed to Aristophanes as much as it did to Miller.

Radical theatre has often proved most powerful when offering the simple solution to a complex question. Aristophanes lived in a world which was not plagued by speculators and multi-national corporations but could still boast its own share of pests, among them warmongers and demagogues. So immediate did his plays appear to their own time that in the years following his death they disappeared from the stage, disqualified by their parochial reference and contemporary targets. This apparent limitation proves to be just the opposite today. While offering a unique picture of life in Athens – the nearest available equivalent to the popular press – hindsight shows Aristophanes pointing to any number of issues and concerns which modern productions have shown to be universal, give or take some local detail.

The growth and development of drama in the ancient world tend to parallel the growth and development of Athens as a cultural and political centre. Of the two major Athenian dramatic festivals, the Lenaia and the Great Dionysia, the Lenaia was dominated by comedy, the Great Dionysia by tragedy, though at one time or another comedies were produced at the Great Dionysia and tragedies at the Lenaia. The Lenaia was the older festival and doubtless from its earliest times, of which there is no record, there was occasion for satirical comment at the expense of local dignitaries and institutions. Such frivolities are part and parcel of the whole idea of holiday. When the deity whose holy day is being celebrated is Dionysos, all the more reason to expect a time of licence, an occasion when restraints will be relaxed and the normal rules of behaviour laid aside. Dionysos was god of wine as well as of the extraordinary, the god of the irrational and the possessed, a fertility and animalistic deity whose variety of functions made him the natural choice to graduate to patronage of a theatre which became a forum for the promulgation of ideas, both serious and subversive.

Tragedy and Comedy were introduced late into the festivals, though competition in music and dance was a formal element from the earliest times. The origins of the Lenaia are lost in the first years of the sixth century BC but something is known about the founding of the Great Dionysia. This was one of the festivals inaugurated by Peisistratos who held autocratic power in Athens until the year 527BC. The decade before his death saw the introduction of tragedy as a new and independent dramatic form at the Great Dionysia, a development credited to Thespis. Aeschylus, the first playwright any of whose work has survived, was probably no more than a year old when Peisistratos was succeeded by his sons Hipparchos and

Hippias. Hipparchos had been assassinated and Hippias sent off into exile, if not oblivion, in Persia ten years before Aeschylus first presented a tragedy at the Great Dionysia. Comedy was only then, about the turn of the century from the sixth to the fifth, recognised as an organised festival entry at the Great Dionysia.

Aeschylus' career as a playwright lasted for over forty years and coincided with the development of democracy. He died in 456BC, ten years before Aristophanes was born. About 442BC Comedy was finally included in competition at the Lenaia. The Peloponnesian War against Sparta broke out in 431 and four years after that, Aristophanes' first play was performed. Chronological detail, of course, is less important than the overall timescale. The upheavals of a hundred and fifty years contributed to the formation of a state which both tolerated and was made uneasy by a genuine political playwright.

Though the Greeks enjoyed an element of competition in many aspects of their festivals, the plays were not originally presented competitively. Nor were any of the practitioners professionals in the sense that they could hope to make a living out of writing or acting. They were to become so, but it was not until the century following the deaths of all the major Athenian playwrights that an actor, still less a dramatist, could have considered himself as a full-time theatre worker. By the end of the fourth century BC a Guild actor could gain more or less permanent employment from appearing at independent festivals throughout the Greek world, from the Middle East to Italy and even North Africa. Many of these Greek communities had their own theatre tradition which stretched back in time, though records of its achievements are sketchy.

Aristotle in the *Poetics* credits Epicharmos and Phormis with the invention of the comic plot in Sicily. Referring to Athens he suggests that 'Comedy was never taken seriously at first and was only granted a chorus by the archon at a late stage' (Ch 5). As an independent form it originated 'in phallic songs, still a feature in a number of our city states' (Ch 4). Old Comedy, it appears now – and it certainly appeared so to Aristotle – was grafted on to festivals which had been celebrating the city and its affairs for years. In other words Old Comedy, however venerable its antecedents, was a product of Athenian democracy: an example, perhaps, of a political system demonstrating its broad-mindedness and parading a willingness to wash even its dirtiest linen in public.

All festival comedy in Athens up to the end of the fifth century BC goes under the label of Old Comedy. Today Old Comedy is represented in extant texts solely by Aristophanes. The names of some of his rivals are known, Kratinos, Eupolis, Ameipsias; so are titles of their plays and quotations from them. Aristophanes was more successful than any of them, though Kratinos had been the man to beat when Aristophanes began his career. Sadly, nothing substantial survives to enable posterity to make its own judgement. The reason is simple enough. Aristophanes was regarded, both in his own time and subsequently, as the best. When the wholesale destruction of texts took place as a result of the various depredations from Alexandria to Byzantium, sufficient copies of Aristophanes were in private hands for the present eleven plays to emerge intact. Some thirty failed to survive along with all the other old comedies of Aristophanes' rivals and predecessors.

Eleven out of forty is a far more representative selection than survives from the work of Aeschylus or Sophocles. Menander, a writer of New Comedy from the further end of the fourth century BC, was little better known than Kratinos until the present century when a number of papyrus fragments were unearthed and what now amounts to two complete plays. As we have them, the eleven Aristophanes plays represent the range of his work from the early *Acharnians* to two late plays, *Ekklesiazousai* or *Women in Power* and *Ploutos* or *Wealth*. These last two reveal such a change of emphasis and tone that they are to be published in a third volume along with the two Menanders whose style they herald.

Nine of Aristophanes' plays have a firm date. The exceptions are *Clouds* – and the text we have is thought to be a revision – and *Thesmophoriazousai*, or *Festival Time*, which was probably presented in 411BC, the same year as *Lysistrata*. The enormous boon this offers is that we have a series of highly political comedies which can be related to known events. The mood of the times and the considerable differences of emphasis are reflected in the texts themselves and the need Aristophanes felt to temper overt criticism with national need. Simultaneously we are in a position to watch the growth in imagination and sureness of touch of a playwright of rare inspiration, the majority of whose work was stimulated by a prolonged and fearful war which was to lead to the disintegration of the Athenian empire.

The Peloponnesian War began in 431BC, when Athenian public life was still dominated by Perikles. Some historians suggest that he hastened it, believing that a confrontation with Sparta and her allies was inevitable and that it would be better conducted under his influence than after his death. As it happened, overcrowding in the city, filled to bursting point with rural refugees from Attika, led to an outbreak of plague to which first Perikles' sons, then he himself fell victim. Far from leading the Athenians towards a glorious victory, his domination of political affairs had been so great that there were no natural successors. Athens found herself a prey to a series of demagogues whose ambition was greater than their ability but who were sharp enough to appreciate how the Assembly might be manipulated to their advantage.

Of these politicians the most powerful, as well as the most strident, was Kleon, a tanner, claimed to be of non-Athenian birth. Of all the stage characters lampooned by Aristophanes only Kleon seems to be truly disliked. In *Knights* Aristophanes presents as singular an attack on one man as any in the history of drama. Apart from any political differences of opinion with Kleon, this real hostility may well date back to Aristophanes' second play *Babylonians*, presented at the Great Dionysia of 426BC.

There he made fun of Kleon as an individual, no offence under Athenian law. Rashly, though, he left himself open to retaliation on a broader count and Kleon took advantage. That we can be so sure of the fine print here is a rare luxury in classical scholarship. On this occasion we have Aristophanes' own reaction. He presented it in his next play, *Acharnians*, the first extant and the first in the present volume.

The leading character of *Acharnians* is Dikaiopolis, an Athenian farmer who decides that after six years of war he has had enough. After acquiring some beggar's props from Euripides, a constant but more affectionate butt, Dikaiopolis asks for the chance to try to convince the Chorus that he is right. In fact he takes the opportunity of addressing the audience, less in the character of Dikaiopolis than as the playwright himself:

> What I say may seem strange, but it's also true,
> And there's no question here of disloyalty,
> As there was last year. Slandering the state, they said,
> In front of strangers. No tourists in tonight.
> No guests. Just you and me. Athenians.
> Cream of the crop. Plus resident aliens, of course.
> As leavening. This is private. Family talk.'

(lines 501-07)

This identification of a major character with playwright is unique in the surviving plays. The notion that the playwright should reveal his own views is not. Usually the mouthpiece is the Chorus who take advantage of a long choral passage to deliver the *parabasis*. *Parabasis* means literally 'a walk forward' or 'a stepping aside', and is a passage of direct address to the audience. All of the plays in the present volume, bar one, do contain a *parabasis*. The exception is *Lysistrata*. Produced in 411BC, with the aftermath of the Sicilian expedition still an open wound and an oligarchic revolution in the offing, this latest demand for peace needed, but perhaps could not risk, the luxury of personal pleading. By the time of the two fourth-century

plays, the *parabasis* has dropped out of the formula alto-
gether, as harsh political comment gives way to more
social comedy and the playwright retreats behind his characters' masks.

The young Aristophanes was ready to take on all comers,
but the experience of *Babylonians* had clearly taught him a
lesson. The significance of Dikaiopolis' remarks relates to
the difference between the two comic festivals, the Lenaia
and the Great Dionysia. The Lenaia was held in the month
of Gamelion, which corresponds more or less to our
January. Nowadays a wet month in Athens and usually the
coldest of the year, it seems at first sight an odd choice.
The programme was shorter and the people were probably
hardier than those of today, but, more importantly, the festival was one which took place in the dead season when
farming, trading and making war were all dormant.

The Great Dionysia by contrast was a spring festival,
held in Elaphebolion, March/April. By this time the sea-
ways were open. Athens, a mercantile nation, was once
more full of visitors from the empire, merchants and political representatives. The city was on display and, in time of
war, the confidence of the city was on the line. For the
playwright who had a comedy to present the option was
open. Offer your play for private consumption or present it
for the world. Though the temptation must have been to
seek an international reputation, there were times when
the sentiments to be expressed would have been too
uncomfortable to share. Not that the state seems to have
exercised direct censorship but Aristophanes, while
declining to pull any public punches, learned to be circum-
spect. Of the plays in this first volume, *Acharnians* and
Knights were Lenaia plays. *Peace* was performed at the
Great Dionysia of 421BC, probably the first time that
Aristophanes had presented a play at the Great Dionysia
since his uncomfortable experience with *Babylonians*.

Lysistrata is something of a special case. The date
assigned to it is 411BC, but that is also the date of *Festival
Time* (included in Plays: Two). Scholarly opinion tends to
put *Lysistrata* as the earlier play, if only by a couple of

months. Any other consideration suggests that if one play was for a restricted audience and one for the whole of Greece, then *Lysistrata* was for the whole of Greece, including, as it does, Spartan as well as Athenian characters. *Festival Time* may be a fine comedy but its setting, a festival exclusive to the women of Athens, would be better suited to the Lenaia.

The argument over which play was produced when and for whom is more than a simple academic question. Aristophanes' forceful comments on current military and political strategy, his attacks on individuals and institutions were not merely a safety valve. In any other society and in any other period of history they would have seemed subversive, bordering upon the treasonable. Only twenty-five years ago in their own native city a repressive government regarded them as such and banned their performance. Within his own time the audacity of Aristophanes is still remarkable. Preaching a doctrine of peace during a war and to an audience composed just as much of those who made policy as of those who were losing family and friends must have given an edge to each year's performance which has had no parallel since.

The stinging satire of British television's *Have I Got News for You* or *Spitting Image*, or BBC Radio's *Week Ending*, may make today's public figures watch or listen in trepidation, dreading that the spotlight will be turned on them, yet dreading still more that it will not, for to be ignored is to be inconspicuous. But in matters of national interest, or when the country's troops are genuinely exposed to danger, different rules apply. During the Gulf War, the BBC withdrew, alongside more obviously sensitive programmes, the film *Carry On Up the Khyber* because it made fun of the British soldier. The theatre in classical Athens had few such qualms.

Giraudoux may for Arthur Miller have created a piece of truly radical theatre. *The Madwoman of Chaillot* certainly aims to undermine the acquisitive and consumerist society that forfeits its values to the pimps of this world.

Aristophanes was prepared to take on institutions as well as individuals in the full knowledge that the authorities and a large proportion of his audience would find his sentiments offensive and unpatriotic. Imagine a *Madwoman* with an anti-military base, set in London, not in 1945 but 1942. Then, perhaps, you have the true taste of Aristophanes, a satirist without favour, without mercy and without fear.

TRANSLATOR'S INTRODUCTION

Aristophanes

Aristophanes is the most kaleidoscopic, most protean of playwrights. Geniality and wit jostle each other, often in the same lines. Satire yields to slapstick, slapstick to parody, parody to lyrical grace. Underlying everything is a lateral view of life, a series of metaphors for the human condition, a precise, poetic vision articulated in pin-sharp images. Aristophanes can remind us, at one time or another, of Rabelais, Jonson, Keats, Laurel and Hardy; he is the father of western comedy, and one of its most dazzling lights.

For several centuries now, the scope outlined above has caused problems. Aristophanes fits none of the scholarly categories for drama: he is a category. In particular, he sits astride the gulf commentators in the last few hundred years have created between 'high' comedy and 'low' comedy. 'High' comedy is text-based, literary, and therefore susceptible to scholarly analysis. In the Middle Ages it became associated with gentility, refinement, good taste – and most of our western comic tradition in 'literature', from Shakespeare to Wilde, from Molière to Frisch, from Sheridan to Albee, pays at least lip-service to this association, either by accepting it or by (gingerly) challenging it. 'Low' comedy, by contrast, is inspirational, topical, and often involves physical as well as verbal skills. It is constantly self-regenerating, and in the Middle Ages it became associated with common (that is, 'vulgar') entertainers: jesters, buffoons, slapstick acrobats and so on. Its history since has been largely separate from 'literary' comedy: circus, music-hall, silent film, stand-up comedy.

The divide is centuries old, and still exists. Plenty of 'mainstream' modern 'comedy' actors are still ignorant of the skills of 'low' comedy. Scholars still tend to ignore or disparage it: dismissing Plautus (say) as 'low' comedy (and somehow therefore inferior to the 'high' comedy of, say,

Terence); devoting reams of paper to explicating *The Beaux' Stratagem* or *The Broken Jug*, some very slim volumes indeed to *An Italian Straw Hat* or *Accidental Death of an Anarchist*, and almost none to the performances of a Will Kempe, a Dan Leno, a Grock or a Lucille Ball. As for comedy which straddles the divide – *commedia dell' arte* springs to mind – it tends to attract lip-service praise from the scholarly establishment and from producers and audiences: admiration unwarmed by either understanding or interest.

It is in this last uneasy category that Aristophanes belongs. There are currently no more than a few dozen Aristophanes scholars, specialists, in the entire world; professional productions of the plays are few and far between, despite the revelation such shows as Karolos Koun's *Birds* can offer, and the enormous pleasure they give. The loss is ours, and it happens because we are shackled by a tradition irrelevant to our author. For Aristophanes and his audience, as for all comedians until the medieval Christian stranglehold on European theatre, there was no gulf at all between 'high' and 'low'. Everything was grist to the humour-mill; Aristophanes used a hundred, a thousand devices – most of them still deployed now, in one comic tradition or another – to provide the blessed balm of laughter.

For all Aristophanes' individual genius, he himself worked within a tradition. It has still only been sketchily restored, but its main ingredients seem to have been scurrilous abuse, fantasy (including the impersonation of animals), slapstick, ritualised arguments, and songs and dances in formal, balancing patterns. All these elements live in Aristophanes' plays. The plot-structure is itself traditional. At the start of each play, the leading character outlines some problem (often political), and decides that the best way to solve it is to undertake some fantastical action, what Dikaiopolis in *Acharnians* calls a 'strange and mighty deed': making a private peace with the enemy, flying to heaven to have it out with Zeus, going to live with the birds, travelling to the Underworld to bring back a poet of the good old school. Often, the hero, in a formal presentation, next has to persuade the Chorus of the wisdom of what he is planning. The deed is then done, often against considerable farcical odds, and the hero triumphs. He is beset by well-wishers and toadies, and reacts with slapstick, before a choral celebration of his victory brings the play to an orgiastic end. Fantasy – or, rather, calm acceptance of the surreal and the absurd – underlies both whole plots and individual events. Scurrility and personal abuse are common, both in the form of instant 'asides', comic jabs to the funny-bone, and in prolonged passages about specific lechers, conmen or perverts. Each play contains such standard passages as the *agon* (a debate-like presentation of the arguments for and against the main issue of the play) and the *parabasis*, in which the Chorus 'step aside' and speak to us about the issues, Aristophanes' merits and the failings of his rivals and political *bêtes-noires*. Impersonation is frequent, sometimes play-long (as with the Choruses of *Wasps* or *Birds*), sometimes fleeting, as when the leading actor in *Wasps* impersonates Odysseus, a judge, a tragic heroine and a drunk. Most plays end with a delirious sequence of song and dance, celebrating the happy outcome of the story. The choruses, and some sequences of dialogue, are in ornate, antiphonal rhythmic patterns – rhythms, we are told, which also underlay the accompanying music and dance-steps. Other traditional elements include prayers, riddles, poems, puns and parodies of well-known sayings and literary tags.

Aristophanes stirs all these ingredients together with relaxed, serene geniality. His view of the world is lateral, and his eye for individual follies is sharp. But more than anything else, the plays are celebrations. They reaffirm what fun it is to be human (unless you are toady, con artist or pervert), and keep up an exuberant, happy flow unmatched in ancient literature – though Homer's *Odyssey* sometimes catches a similar mood. Aristophanes is also a master of staging. Scholarly controversy here is a minefield, but it seems likely that Aristophanes used a simple setting, often just an open space with two doors, and that he played every conceivable variation on the available effects, from the crane to the *ekkuklema* ('roll-out': see note 4, page 258), from extravagant costumes to slapstick dance. In the eleven extant plays there are three stage directions only – 'Someone plays a flute' is typical. It is, however, apparent from the texts when most exits and entrances take place, and indeed when some specific action or effect is intended. We can clearly see, from the words spoken, that Trygaios in *Peace* flies to the gods on a dung-beetle, that in *Frogs* lines from plays are weighed on scales, or that Mnesilochos in *Festival Time* tries to hide his phallus from the women who suspect that he is not the 'mother of nine' he claims to be. By and large, the fewer and plainer the stage directions in a translation, the better. (This is a fine statement, which I have found it hard at times to live up to. In *Peace*, especially, some lines are incomprehensible unless specific 'business' is described.)

Two other elements, crucial to the Aristophanic mix, are bawdy and politics. There are many different levels of bawdy, from straightforward use of 'four-letter' words (in Greek, often eight- or nine-letter words) to double, triple and quadruple entendre. Bawdy is sometimes ironical, sometimes at the level of the playground, sometimes (as in the Megarian scene in *Acharnians*) the motor of the satire. In all cases, it caused Aristophanes' reputation enormous harm in the Puritan era. Emasculation became a standard feature of texts and translations – in my opinion, unforgivably. Aristophanes' sexuality and scatology are innocent and inoffensive; they can be left to fend for themselves.

The second element, politics, poses problems of a different kind. Aristophanes' politics are specific to Athens, to his own time; he continually refers to people and events of which most modern readers and audiences have never heard. The plays in the present volume are particularly crammed with political references of this kind. This is because they were performed during the Peloponnesian War (431-404BC), during which the harmony between

Athens and Sparta, which had allowed them to lead the
united Greek states against the Persians some sixty years
before, was replaced by bloody and apparently unresolv-
able conflict, as destructive to the spirit as civil war.
Aristophanes' attitude, in all the war plays, is that no one
benefits from this except frauds and self-glorifying politicians (particularly Kleon, the abrasive leader from 427BC
to his death five years later, and his toadies). Upstart
lawyers, informers and armchair soldiers proliferate.
Those who suffer are the ordinary people: good old men
who fought the Persians at Marathon and are now reduced
to penury; farmers whose fields have been wrecked by
invading armies; mothers whose sons have marched away
to death.

Although Aristophanes' specific references may seem
arcane, the types, problems and proposed solutions in his
plays are universal. It is unnecessary to update instances
(for example to the US Civil War or the 'troubles' in
Ireland) to make the action comprehensible. In this translation, I have left most references intact, adding a few
words of explanation if necessary. (For study purposes,
end-notes and the Who's Who give extra detail.) With
political jokes, as with everything else, I think that we can
trust our author.

My work on this translation, already a pleasure, was
made even more enjoyable by the encouragement of
friends. I should like especially to thank the late William
Arrowsmith (whose own, American-flavour translations
offer a mark of quality to aim at), Kenneth Dover, Frederic
Raphael, Michael Walton and above all Valerie McLeish. I
offer the book to Frederic Raphael, in thanks for twenty
years' warm friendship.

Acharnians

Acharnians was first produced at the Lenaia in January,
425BC. It won first prize. It was the third of Aristophanes'
plays to be produced, and is the first to survive. He was in
his early twenties. The play was produced not in his name,

but in that of Kallistratos (backer? leading actor? fellow-writer?); Aristophanes gives reasons for this in *Knights* (lines 512ff).

425BC was some half-dozen years into the Peloponnesian War. Every year until then, the Spartans had invaded Athenian territory, devastating the country areas and causing a panic influx of farming families to the safety of the city. (It was not actually all *that* safe: in 430 plague killed one quarter of the population.) However, in 425 an earthquake prevented invasion, causing something of a lull – and giving an opportunity, perhaps, for the citizens to take stock of what had happened in the war so far, strategically, politically and ethically. This was the atmosphere in which Aristophanes wrote, and in which his play won its prize. He focuses on the plight of villagers forced to live in the uncongenial city: Dikaiopolis, a yeoman farmer; the fire-eating charcoal-burners of Acharnai. He inveighs against Kleon, Lamachos and other members of the war-faction – not to mention the slurry of bureaucrats, placemen and informers who bob in their wake. But the Lenaia (the January festival at which the play was produced, too early in the year for sea-visitors to Athens, and therefore attended chiefly by native Athenians: 'family') also gave him the chance for some free speech unprecedented even by his standards. The care with which Dikaiopolis prepares for his big speech, and the atmosphere of risk surrounding its delivery, still crackle from the lines – and the reason is that he was defending the Spartans, asserting their common humanity with Athenians, in a way hardly in tune with the mood of the times. This, added to Aristophanes' robust but sympathetic treatment of the Megarian and Theban (disgraced former allies of Athens) move the play into decidedly risky comic territory.

For all its long-lost topicality and political urgency, *Acharnians* is still one of Aristophanes' freshest, most accessible plays. The reason is faultless, almost casual, technical brilliance. Aristophanes' basic plot-idea (Dikaiopolis' 'strange and mighty deed', the private peace) is a simple but sound platform on which he builds a tower of ever-greater absurdity, each scene effortlessly topping the one before. The parodies – of an Assembly dominated by rogues and fools; of Euripides' high-tragic style – are superbly carried off, funny even to those who know nothing of the originals. Dikaiopolis' big speech, ostensibly about the Spartans, is universal in feeling, as is the heartfelt private festival with which he celebrates his peace. The *alazones* ('sponger') scenes give splendid opportunities for slapstick, and for dialect comedians. Above all, *Acharnians* offers an amazing display of linguistic and rhythmic fire-works. If Sophocles' *Oidipous Tyrannos* is the very model of an 'Aristotelian' tragedy, a kind of template for the form, then *Acharnians* could serve the same function for comedy. The *agon*, *parabasis*, *alazones* scenes and *komos* are fine exam-ples of how each should be written, and there is hardly a speech, hardly a line, which is not (a) precisely to the recipe and (b) seemingly spontaneous and original. In par-ticular, the formal dialogues between Dikaiopolis and Lamachos demonstrate the maxim that adherence to rules can liberate the imagination – demonstrate it as tri-umphantly as does Bach's *Art of Fugue*.

The play's staging requires a large open space (in the original, the Pnyx hill where the Assembly met), with the doors of three houses: those of Dikaiopolis, Lamachos and Euripides. The Euripides scene makes use of the *ekkuk-lema*, allowing us to glimpse the maestro at work on his 'high tragedies'. (See lines 395ff, and note 4, page 258.) *Acharnians* requires a huge number of silent extras. The constant arrival of new characters, no less than cocky lin-guistic flow, exuberant plotting and political acuity, must have been a main contributory factor in the play's success.

Knights

Knights was first produced at the Lenaia in January, 424BC, and won first prize. Aristophanes was in his early twenties. *Knights* was the first of his plays to be presented in his own name – as he explains in the *parabasis*, lines 498ff. There is a tradition that no other actor was willing to play Paphlagon/Kleon, so he took the part himself. (He may also have been attracted by the sheer juiciness of the role.) Stringencies of casting (or a miserly backer?) may also account for the general compactness of the play. It has five characters only, a handful of extras (compared to the army required for, say, *Acharnians* or *Birds*), and a single, unified Chorus. The music- and dance-numbers are, by and large, self-contained, able to be rehearsed separately from the main action. Few Athenian comedies (or tragedies) are so easy to mount – if you can find actors able to play the two main roles.

Knights is a one-dimensional play, and its dimension is caricature. There is nothing ironical here: the play shouts with the raucous vigour of a fairground barker. It contains some of Aristophanes' crudest, coarsest jokes, and its political commentary (the most overt in all his surviving work) is rammed home with all the delicacy of a Hogarth, a Gillray or a Gerald Scarfe. The rumbustuousness of the action sweeps all before it; even now, when topicality is lost, *Knights* throbs with theatrical energy, an entertainment as engulfing and irresistible as circus.

Four of the characters are caricatures of real people. Demos ('the People') stands for all the citizens of Athens. He is complacent and stupid, and is incompetently served by two equally brainless slaves called Nikias and Demosthenes (two leading generals at this point in the Peloponnesian War). He, and they, are under the thumb of a loud-mouthed, lying bully called Paphlagon (literally 'the man from Paphlagonia', but punning on *paphlazon*, 'foaming at the mouth'). To the audience, Paphlagon was clearly Kleon, the forceful, touchy war-leader with whom Aristophanes had often crossed swords before. Forcefulness and touchiness are the only qualities of the 'real' Kleon parodied in the play – except for one real event, which somehow intrudes into the action at every point. This was (the real) Kleon's recent success at Pylos. A group of Spartans had been blockaded (by the real general Demosthenes) on a tiny island off the coast at Pylos. Kleon had refused to allow surrender, and so end the war; instead, he took over from Demosthenes, dealt with the Spartans and claimed the credit. While many Athenians treated this as a significant victory over an implacable enemy, others (including Aristophanes) proclaimed Kleon's motives as corrupt as his methods.

This event apart, the politics of the play are entirely caricature. And just as it is an axiom of political philosophy that a state should seek its rulers from the best citizens available, so in the cartoon-politics of *Knights* the opposite applies. The only way to get rid of Paphlagon/Kleon is to find someone even worse. Thus we are presented with the wholly imaginary character Agorakritos ('Choice of the market-place'), a seller of guts and tripe whose venality, crudeness and slyness smother even Paphlagon's, and whose final winning *coup* is a spectacular repeat of (the real) Kleon's sleight of hand over (the real) Demosthenes at Pylos. Agorakritos is one of Aristophanes' finest parts: a swaggering braggart delighted with himself and the role he plays, a very Falstaff of the common man.

Although *Knights* follows the basic structure of Old Comedy, it is in effect a continuous *agon*, a prolonged contest from start to finish. Each 'round' takes a different tack, but each drives us further towards the ultimate goal, the displacing of Paphlagon. In this play, comic abuse and physical slapstick reach delirious heights. Few pieces of drama leave the audience so breathless. Aristophanes claimed that his attacks on Kleon, in this and earlier plays, were regarded as daring even by the outspoken standards of Athenian comedy. Even so, the play had no apparent effect on the career or style of the real-life Kleon. He remained in power, and his method and manner of politics hardly changed. Perhaps he enjoyed Aristophanes' mockery – many modern politicians are said to ask for signed copies of even the most savage cartoons made against them. Perhaps we are wrong to expect satire to change the world. As Philip Roth points out (writing about his own lampoon of the Richard Nixon US administration, *Our Gang*), 'Writing satire is a literary, not a political act, however volcanic the reformist or even revolutionary passion in the author. Satire is moral rage transformed into comic art.' When the comedy is done, the politician, the Kleon, can serenely go on doing exactly as he or she has done before; the comedian, by contrast, has to move on to new targets, to a fresh barrage of jokes.

In common with its general structural simplicity, *Knights* needs nothing in the way of staging except a single doorway. The original setting was the Pnyx hill, where the Athenian Assembly met: it is here that Aristophanes imagines Demos, 'the People', having his house.

Peace

Peace was first produced at the Great Dionysia in late March or early April, 421BC, and won second prize. Aristophanes was in his mid-twenties.

The Great Dionysia was a five-day, public festival in honour of Dionysos, involving processions, rituals, and competitions in music, dance and drama. It came each year soon after the sea was fit for merchant ships, and the city was accordingly crammed with visitors. The atmosphere may have been analogous to that on a big modern religious occasion (a mixture, as it were, of the Doge's marriage with the sea in Venice and the Hindu Holi festival), with the city's private rituals (instituted by Peisistratos to re-enact the god Dionysos' arrival in Athens) being performed before the gaze of a wider public. And the festivities of 421BC may well have been especially ecstatic. The Peace of Nikias – the first substantial suspension of hostilities since the Peloponnesian War began a decade before – had either just been signed or was about to be so, and the political atmosphere must have been charged with an utterly different kind of optimism from the gung-ho military certainties of earlier years.

In fact the political and military situation was one of stand-off. Both Sparta and Athens had fought to the point of near-exhaustion. All initiatives had failed; every triumph had been balanced with disaster; both Kleon, the Athenian war-leader, and Brasidas, the chief Spartan general, had been killed without leaving obvious successors; both states were near financial ruin. In retrospect – and despite the public excitement it probably caused while Aristophanes' play was in rehearsal – the Peace of Nikias was really no more than an interlude, the rest-point between two rounds of a brutal title-fight.

Perhaps the delicacy of the situation accounts for the style of *Peace*. Its politics are notably less specific and contentious than those of Aristophanes' earlier plays. It addresses, rather, a kind of general yearning for stability, replacing specific *ad hominem* attacks with the advocacy of pan-Hellenic unity, of an outburst of common humanity to finish the job politicians and generals have failed to do. The Chorus includes representatives from all the main states involved in the war. The contest in the play is not partisan, but between the advocates and beneficiaries of peace and war – and in context, it is no contest at all. For the first time in his surviving work, Aristophanes reveals his lyrical powers. The choruses praising the blessings of peace are some of the sunniest and most graceful lines he ever wrote – and they have a feeling of yearning, of urgency, which must have chimed exactly with the mood of at least some of the watching crowd.

Peace is also notable for its slapstick. The central ideas, flying to heaven and physically rescuing Peace from a hole, are embodied in a series of ludicrous and hilarious sight gags, beginning with the dung-beetle, continuing with the Chorus tugging on the ropes, and proceeding to the Slave's reactions to the arrival of Peace and her nubile attendants in Trygaios' farmyard. The gods are presented with the sure farce-touch Aristophanes also deploys for them in *Frogs*, *Birds* and *Wealth*: he had a particular fondness for the epicene Hermes – or for the actor who played him? The sponger-scenes are often dismissed by scholars as perfunctory, but in fact each carries through a single gag-idea (putting armour and weapons to absurd domestic uses; sending up war-songs; sending off beggar-priests) with almost epigrammatic verve. The final procession is, in stage terms, a gloriously appropriate conclusion to a play whose whole impetus has been from darkness to light, from uncertainty to celebration. Far from being the perfunctory, cobbled-together job some scholars claim, *Peace* is one of Aristophanes' most carefully-constructed, 'achieved' plays – and the fact that its success is theatrical rather than literary is, despite scholarly sniffs, no handicap. What else should one ask of plays?

The staging requires an open space, with a central opening (through which Peace will be drawn) and a doorway at either side: Trygaios' house and the entrance to Heaven. Beside Trygaios' house is a building resembling a stable or large pig-sty (in Athens, made from wickerwork): the dung-beetle's home. Some scholars have suggested that the Heaven scenes take place on an upper level, that Trygaios 'flies' from the theatre floor to the roof of the stage-building. But there is no need for this. The crane may well have carried him not up but in a lurching arc from one side of the stage to the other – a journey paralleled in *Frogs*, when Dionysos travels by boat from Athens to the Underworld.

Lysistrata

Lysistrata was first produced in 411BC, the same year as *Festival Time* (*Thesmophoriazousai*). Aristophanes was in his mid-thirties. No one knows whether the play was performed at the Lenaia or the Great Dionysia, or what prize it won. Tradition says that it appeared at the Lenaia; but to modern eyes the play seems to have a more general, more pan-Hellenic, relevance than *Festival Time*, and so to be more suitable for the huge Great Dionysia.

By 411, it must have seemed to the beleaguered Athenians that the Peloponnesian War would never end. It had been the focus of their lives for two decades, and the conditions which had once seemed a temporary nightmare – overcrowding in the city; jumped-up loudmouths in political and military charge; informers – had become the continuum of daily life. Hundreds of thousands of young men had been killed: there can have been hardly a family in Athens without cause to grieve. Specific national catastrophes had made things worse, not better. In 415BC the Athenians had mounted a huge, almost vainglorious, expedition to overwhelm Sparta's allies in Sicily – and their fleet, the city's glory for over half a century, had been destroyed. Loss of the fleet had led to defection by many of Athens' allies, and the Spartans had made a useful alliance with the huge Persian Empire. The situation was not hopeless, but the best possibility for Athens must have seemed simply to struggle on in the hope of some unforeseen, unforeseeable, change of tactics or fortune.

Such a change is precisely what Lysistrata proposes. To the largely-male audience at the first performance, her plan would have seemed as bizarre as it does to the Commissioner in the play. At this time, in Athens, there was hot debate not so much about the nature of women's intelligence, as about its very existence. The (male) consensus was that women simply had no capacity for abstract thought; they were incapable of logic, unable to see wider issues, not to be trusted with anything but domestic matters. Nowadays, thanks to our Puritan heritage, we in the west tend to think that the outrage caused by the play is due to the sex-strike; to the Athenian audience, the idea of handing state affairs to women would have caused even louder gasps. In fact, the sex-strike is really no more than slapstick decoration to the main argument, the metaphor which fuels the farce – and to make it work, Aristophanes cheerfully ignores any 'real-life' alternative sexual possibilities open to Athenian men. They would have considered the sight of a gaggle of women (or rather, travesty-actors) on-stage as inherently hilarious – and this feeling is essential for Aristophanes' point to be made, when the same empty-headed women outwit, out-think and outflank the men. And yet, unlike (say) Euripides' *Women of Troy*, which also uses a wide range of travesty-acting to give edge to serious ethical and moral points about war, *Lysistrata* never reaches beyond the superficial meaning of the stage-picture. It is not a play about female and male attitudes to the opposite sex, to public affairs or to war and peace; it is a farce about erections. Despite the 'female' cast, the play's tone is determinedly masculine. Its linguistic style is brittle and terse; its jokes attack head-on; from start to finish it is a parade rather than a seduction.

In stage technique, *Lysistrata* makes a break with Aristophanes' earlier surviving plays. In all of them, from *Acharnians* to *Peace*, from *Knights* to *Clouds*, he followed the same basic formulas of construction and style, with variations to suit the needs of each particular plot. Even *Birds*, the most complex of his earlier surviving plays (written some three years before *Lysistrata*), observes the conventional patterns of *agon*, *parabasis*, *alazones* scenes and *komos*: they are extended and amplified, but the underlying structure is the same as in *Acharnians* of a dozen years earlier. In *Lysistrata*, by contrast, the conventions begin to dissolve before our eyes. There is an *agon*, but it is an argument less between two specific 'sides' than between several points of view – Lysistrata and the women; Lysistrata and the Commissioner; the male and female Choruses – and the issues are not resolved each time, merely broken off and later resumed, until the moment when the male and female Choruses unite, or even until the suite of dances which ends the play. *Alazones* scenes are not grouped in the second half, as usual, but punctuate the action and carry it on: the scene of the women's escape attempts, and the Myrrhine-Kinesias scene, in particular, have essential dynamic force. (The Myrrhine-Kinesias scene also breaks the *alazon*-scene pattern in another way: the play's leading character is not involved.) Above all, Aristophanes uses the Chorus in ways unprecedented in his (extant) output, and equalled (by coincidence?) only in his other surviving plays involving a large group of women, *Festival Time*

(*Thesmophoriazousai*) and *Women in Power* (*Ekklesiazousai*). The entry of the Chorus is preceded by the arrival of a group of women, some speaking individual parts, some silent extras. The Chorus itself is divided into two hostile groups, which come together in standard fashion, but then seem to divide again, changing their identity from old women and old men to Spartan and Athenian dancers. (Or were these a new Chorus, of speciality dancers?) Throughout, the Chorus is integrated into the action, and propels it as well as reacting to it: something which confounds the 'rules'. There is a 'company' articulation to this play which sets it apart from Aristophanes' previous surviving work (in which the hierarchy of protagonist and subordinate actors is crucial). In later plays, he developed 'integrated' structures further, in different ways; technical rawness here may be a sign that *Lysistrata* was something of an experiment.

The play's staging is controversial. It is set outside the entrance to the Akropolis, and requires only one central doorway (perhaps representing the ornate Propylaia whose ruins still survive). Some scholars say that the women, occupying the Akropolis, appeared on an upper level, and the men, trying to force entrance, appeared on the stage floor. But there is no evidence for this, and the action can be staged just as easily with all performers on the same level.

Note: line-numbers alongside the texts relate to the Greek original rather than to the translation. Superior numbers in the texts refer to notes at the end of the book.

ACHARNIANS

Characters

DIKAIOPOLIS
SERGEANT
AMPHITHEOS
AMBASSADORS
PSEUDARTABAS
HIS EXCELLENCY
DIKAIOPOLIS' DAUGHTER
KEPHISOPHON
EURIPIDES
LAMACHOS
MEGARIAN
HIS DAUGHTERS
NIKARCHOS
THEBAN
LAMACHOS' AIDE DE CAMP
TOWN CRIER
YOKEL
BEST MAN

silent parts:

AMBASSADORS
BAGPIPERS
BRIDESMAID
CITIZENS
DANCING-GIRLS
DIKAIOPOLIS' WIFE
EUNUCHS
THE FEARSOME FIRM
ISMENIAS (the Theban's slave)
OFFICIALS
ORDERLIES
POLICE OFFICERS
SLAVES
XANTHIAS (Dikaiopolis' slave)

CHORUS OF CHARCOAL-BURNERS FROM
ACHARNAI

Athens. Pnyx Hill: a large open space where the Assembly meets. At
the sides, doors to the houses of DIKAIOPOLIS *and* LAMACHOS.
DIKAIOPOLIS *is waiting.*

DIKAIOPOLIS.
This isn't funny. I'm hurt, deep down inside.
Not much to laugh at. This and that. Four things.
But troubles: a sand-dune, a desert, grain by grain.
You know what really made me jump up and down?
That court case, in the comedy last year.
Prime Minister Kleon against the People.
He gobbled bribes; they sued; he spewed.
Democracy in action. I enjoyed that. Thanks.
But then – a really tragic blow. I flew
To the theatre, beak open, panting for Aeschylus,   10
And what was playing? Theognis!
Heart attack time: that nearly *was* a tragedy.
Good news: the harp competition ended early –
And they slipped in one of those herdboy's songs.
Not like yesterday! I died, I went cross-eyed
When Chairis struck up those marches. *Sideways?*
But today's the worst of all. I've been cut up before –
I've been shaving a long time – but never like this.
They called a full Assembly, here, today,
And where is everybody? Somewhere else.   20
Gabbing and gossiping. No time for state affairs.
Democracy in action? Huh! Their Worships –
The Chairman, the Tellers, the Secretary –
Where are they? Don't worry, they'll soon be here,
Jostling and tumbling like a river in spate.
And for what? To discuss making peace with Sparta?
You're joking. To claim their front-row seats.
O Athens, Athens! I'm always first. I find a seat –
No problem there – I wait here on my own,
I groan, I yawn, I stretch, I fart, I'm bored,   30
I scribble, scratch, do sums in my head,
I think about my farm, I long for peace.
City life: I hate it. I want my village.
No salesmen there, no 'Buy! Buy! Buy!' –
It's share and share alike, it's bye-bye, 'Buy!'
Well, here I am. I'm ready. Start when you like.

I'll heckle and clap and shout
If anyone talks of anything but peace.
40   Aha! Their Worships, here at last.
Late afternoon. I told you: look. Fighting,
Falling over each other for the same best seat.

Enter OFFICIALS *and* CITIZENS, *directed by the*
SERGEANT.

SERGEANT.
Move forward.
Don't cross the official line.

Enter AMPHITHEOS.

AMPHITHEOS.
Am I in time?

SERGEANT.
All motions through the Chair.
Who makes a motion?

AMPHITHEOS.
I do.

SERGEANT.
Name?

AMPHITHEOS.
Amphitheos.

SERGEANT.
Human?

AMPHITHEOS.
No, divine.
Triptolemos begat Amphitheos (the First);
Amphitheos begat Keleos; Keleos begat Lykinos;
Lykinos married Phainarete (my Mummy)
50   And begat Amphitheos (the Second): me.
I'm one of *them*. A god. Divine.
They sent me here to organise the peace
Between you and Sparta. I've full authority –

But what I haven't got is my expenses.
Something about red tape. I *said* I was a god.

SERGEANT.
Guards! Throw him out.

AMPHITHEOS.
Help! Keleos! Triptolemos!

DIKAIOPOLIS.
Just a minute. Your Worships! Through the Chair!
What's going on? It's peace he's offering.
He says we can hang up our shields.

SERGEANT.
Sit down. Shut up.

DIKAIOPOLIS.
I won't. I move a motion: peace.   60

SERGEANT.
The ambassadors from Persia.

Enter AMBASSADORS, *with* PSEUDARTABAS
and his EUNUCHS.

DIKAIOPOLIS.
Persia! Just look at them.
Peacocks and parakeets. They make me puke.

SERGEANT.
Shut *up*.

DIKAIOPOLIS.
What *are* they wearing?

AMBASSADOR.
Athenians, countrymen, long months ago
We set off, for you, to Persian lands afar.
Two drachmas a day, expenses.

DIKAIOPOLIS.
Poor old drachs.

AMBASSADOR.
> For you, with tireless tread we ploughed the
> plains;
70   For you, we sat and suffered in silk sedans;
> Each caravanserai we had to try –

DIKAIOPOLIS.
> You should have been here, at home with me.
> Guard-duty. Battlements, doss in the dog-dirt –

AMBASSADOR.
> Oh, those feasts! Those neverending feasts!
> Glass goblets...gold...
> No water to drink, just wine, wine, wine.
> So wearisome.

DIKAIOPOLIS.
> Athenians, countrymen,
> I'll tell you what's wearisome...

AMBASSADOR.
> To be the boast of Barbary, the toast
> Of the Tuareg, you must eat and drink the most.

DIKAIOPOLIS.
> So what's the secret *here*? Big bum? Big dick?

AMBASSADOR.
80   Four years dragged by. We reached the palace,
> His Highness' hallowed halls. He wasn't there.
> On manoeuvres. With his army, the Immortals.
> Eight months in the High Hills, the Pearly Peaks.
> They called it 'Operation Shitabrick'.

DIKAIOPOLIS.
> Takes time. You've got to work it out.

AMBASSADOR.
> His Majesty came home. He welcomed us.
> Bestowed his bounty. A banquet.
> Bull shish-kebab, spit-roasted, whole.

DIKAIOPOLIS.
  That *is* a lot of bull.

AMBASSADOR.
  To follow: pheasant. Extremely pleasant.
  Huge great drumsticks. May have been ostrich.

DIKAIOPOLIS.
  Or total quack. Two drachs a day – for this!   90

AMBASSADOR.
  And now we're home. But not alone. We bring
  Pseudartabas, His Majesty's Great Eye.

DIKAIOPOLIS.
  Oh ay, his eye.

SERGEANT.
  His Majesty's Great Eye.

  The EUNUCHS *reveal* PSEUDARTABAS.

DIKAIOPOLIS.
  What *does* he look like? Some kind of fishing boat?
  Hey, sailor, over here. Put into port,
  Ship oars, drop anchor, step ashore, get stuffed.

AMBASSADOR.
  Pseudartabas, Magnificence, Proud Prince,
  Deign to address us. His Majesty's Own Words.

PSEUDARTABAS.
  Iyarta man exarxan apissona satra.¹   100

AMBASSADOR.
  D'you get it?

DIKAIOPOLIS.
  No.

AMBASSADOR.
  He says His Majesty is sending gold.
  Once more, Magnificence. Like this. 'Gold.' 'Gold.'

PSEUDARTABAS.
  Stuff youlot. Noget gold.

DIKAIOPOLIS.
  Well, that was clear enough.

AMBASSADOR.
  Translate, then.

DIKAIOPOLIS.
  No need.
  'Stuff you lot. No get gold.'

AMBASSADOR.
  No no. We'll get *hold* of the *stuff*, he said.
  Nuggets.

DIKAIOPOLIS.
110   You're dreaming. Here, let me.

  (*to* PSEUDARTABAS)

  Oi, Pissonya! See this? Give me a straight answer,
  Or get a knuckle sandwich. This Great Big King,
  Is he really going to send us gold?

  PSEUDARTABAS *nods his head. The* EUNUCHS
  shake theirs.

  So the ambassador's a liar?

  PSEUDARTABAS *shakes his head. The* EUNUCHS
  nod.

  There's something here that's queer.
  One nods, two shake; two nod, one shakes.
  These eunuchs...too familiar.
  I know this one, for a start:
  It's Kleisthenes from up the road. Look, fool!
  You've shaved down there but not up here.
120   And you –
  Who's underneath this getup? Straton! *Well!*

SERGEANT.
  Shut up. Sit down. The authorities invite
  The Great King's Eye to lunch.

DIKAIOPOLIS.
It's suicide time.
I get to hang about. They get free lunch.
There's nothing else for it:
I'll have to do a strange and mighty deed.
Amphitheos. Psst! Amphitheos.

AMPHITHEOS.
What?

DIKAIOPOLIS.
Take these eight drachmas. Go to Sparta,   130
Buy a treaty – for me, the old woman and the kids.
The rest of you can go on playing charades:
I'm privatising peace.

Exit AMPHITHEOS.

SERGEANT.
Pray silence for His Excellency, here
To report on his fact-finding tour Up North.

Enter HIS EXCELLENCY.

HIS EXCELLENCY.
Friends...

DIKAIOPOLIS.
Another fraud.

HIS EXCELLENCY.
We lingered long Up North. We had our reasons.

DIKAIOPOLIS.
Sticky fingers.

HIS EXCELLENCY.
Snow, friends, snow on snow on snow.
I just won't mention ice.

DIKAIOPOLIS.
How nice.   140

HIS EXCELLENCY.
We spent this time drinking with Lord Sitalkes.
Lord, how he loves you all!

'Up Athens!' he used to say. 'Howway the lads!'
We gave his son, a likely lad,
Freedom of the city. We promised him a feast
As soon as he arrived. He fell on his knees
(The lad) and begged his Dad to send you men.
'I'll do it, lad, by Gad,' the Daddy said –
He was sacrificing at the time. 'I'll send
150   Them men all right. A shoal! A school!'

DIKAIOPOLIS.
    I knew this was fishy.

HIS EXCELLENCY.
    The vanguard's just outside.
    Hand-picked for action.

DIKAIOPOLIS.
    Told you.

SERGEANT.
    Northerners, atten-SHUN! Quick, MARCH!

Enter THE FEARSOME FIRM.

DIKAIOPOLIS.
    Who are these?

HIS EXCELLENCY.
    The Fearsome Firm.

DIKAIOPOLIS.
    You're joking. *Firm? This* one?
    D'you call *that* firm?

HIS EXCELLENCY.
    No, no, be fair. Two drachmas a day,
160   And they'll conquer the world for you.

DIKAIOPOLIS.
    Two drachs,
    To these apologies, to these limp pricks?

THE FEARSOME FIRM *makes a sortie*.

Hey! Dammit, they've pinched my ploughman's.
Put that down. It's mine.

HIS EXCELLENCY.
Careful! If they've tasted onion...

DIKAIOPOLIS.
Your Worships! Don't just sit there!
Chair! I'm being mugged in my own backyard –
And by northerners. Ah, the hell with it.
I veto the Assembly. No more negotiations.   170
I've had an omen. I felt a drop of rain.

Pandemonium.

SERGEANT.
Northerners go home. Come back tomorrow.
Their Worships declare the Assembly closed.

Exeunt all but DIKAIOPOLIS.

DIKAIOPOLIS.
I was really looking forward to that lunch.
Ah, here's Amphitheos, from Sparta. Hi.

Enter AMPHITHEOS, *breathless.*

AMPHITHEOS.
Can't stop. Can't talk. Acharnians.

DIKAIOPOLIS.
Pardon?

AMPHITHEOS.
I was on my way here, with the treaties.
These. Some old men sniffed me out.
Charcoal-burners. Battle-veterans. Acharnians.   180
Tough as army boots. 'Oi, come back here, you
    swine!'
They shouted. 'Making treaties with Sparta.
What about our vines – the ones they burned and
    slashed?'
They started picking up stones. I legged it. Fast.
They're after me. Can't you hear them? Listen!

DIKAIOPOLIS.
Never mind *them*. Where are the treaties?

AMPHITHEOS.
Here. There are three to choose from, all vintage.
How d'you fancy this? A five-year truce.

He uncorks a small wine-flask. DIKAIOPOLIS *sniffs.*

DIKAIOPOLIS.
Puah.

AMPHITHEOS.
What's wrong?

DIKAIOPOLIS.
190   It stinks of shipyards, caulking, tar.

AMPHITHEOS.
Try this. A ten-year truce.

Same business with a medium-sized flask.

DIKAIOPOLIS.
No. Missions to foreigners...put the case...
Make allies...gather contributions. No.

AMPHITHEOS.
This one then: a thirty-year truce, by sea and land.

Same business with a huge flask.

DIKAIOPOLIS.
This is the one. It's happy hour!
What does it smell of? Nectar, ambrosia,
No more army rations. Look, here on the label:
'Stand down, feel free.' I'll take it,
I'll pour, I'll drink –
200   And your Acharnians can go to Hell.
I'm free of war. I've got my peace.
It's celebration time.

He goes into his house.

AMPHITHEOS.
  But not for me.
  Here come the Acharnians. I'm off.

  Exit. Enter CHORUS.

CHORUS.
  This way! Hurry! Hunt him down.
  Where? Ask. Wait! Don't lose me.
  Track him! Trip him! Catch the clown.
  Ladies and gentlemen, excuse me:
  Did that treaty-snaffler sneak this way?
  If he did, he'll pay!

  I'm old, I'm tired, there's hardly a hint   210
  Of the old days. *Then*, I was Number One:
  The hundred yards, the dash, the sprint –
  Now it's all dead and done.
  No more first past the post: 220
  I'm a hasbeen, a ghost.

  Catch the fast bastard! Don't let him go.
  He talks to those apes
  Who hurt us so.
  They vandalise our vines, they grab our grapes.
  Make him sorry. Throw stones.   230
  Catch your quarry. Break bones.

DIKAIOPOLIS (*inside*).
  Peace! Peace!
  Make way for peace.

CHORUS.
  It's the treaty-nabber. Quick!
  He's holding a procession.
  We'll teach him a lesson.
  Hide here. He makes me sick.   240

  A procession comes out of DIKAIOPOLIS' *house:*
  DIKAIOPOLIS' DAUGHTER, *with a loaf held high,*
  DIKAIOPOLIS' WIFE, *carrying a breadboard,* XANTHIAS

holding an enormous, phallic sunshade, two girl
SLAVES *with sticks and a firepot²*.

DIKAIOPOLIS.
Make way for peace. Make way.
Loaf-bearer, lead. A step in front.
Xanthias, get that thing straight.
Line up over there. Let's start.

DAUGHTER.
Give me the breadboard, Mummy.
I *know* what to do. I'll use my loaf.

DIKAIOPOLIS.
That's right. Dionysos, lord,
Bless our procession, our sacrifice,
Here with our family about us, our slaves,
250   As we hold our private celebration
And our guard-duty days are done.
A thirty-year peace by sea and land –
O help me, help me make the best of it.
Loaf-bearer, lift. Say cheese.
Pussy-cat! What a lucky man he'll be,
Who marries you, kittens you,
Gives you a litter of lovelies,
Fumbling and farting in the hay all day.
So like their Mummy. Aah! Walk round.
Show the audience. And you lot, watch it.
No toying with her tassels.
260   Xanthias, follow. *Up*, man, up!
I'll walk behind; I'll sing the song.
Wife, watch from upstairs. Admire.
Is everyone ready? Go.

Come down, O lord. Our wars are done.
It's time for fun.
It's time to dance, it's time to prance,
It's party-time.

For five long, weary, war-torn years
You closed your ears

To thuds and thumps and battle-cries.
You hid your eyes.

But now, stuff Lamachos. Look, there: 270
That pretty pair.
One stirs the fire; one feeds the flame.
They'll play your game.

So, bottoms up! Our wars are done.
It's time for fun.
It's time to dance, it's time to prance,
It's party-time.

CHORUS.
That's him! Got him!   280
Smash him!
Stone the bastard!
Bash him!

DIKAIOPOLIS.
You'll crush my cup.

CHORUS.
We'll beat you up.

DIKAIOPOLIS.
I'm innocent.

CHORUS.
You're twisted, bent.
Treaty-maker! Athens-hater!   290
Spartan-lover! Traitor!

DIKAIOPOLIS.
I *can* explain.

CHORUS.
No! Howl with pain.

DIKAIOPOLIS.
I'll tell you why.

CHORUS.
Don't even try.
You'll lose:

300   We'll skin you alive
      For shoes.
      You're not going to thrive.
      You'll be black, you'll be blue, you'll be tartan;
      You'll be sorry you ever turned Spartan.

DIKAIOPOLIS.
      Stop foaming at the mouth. Whoa. Steady.
      I'll prove I was right. Are you ready?

CHORUS.
      Speak up for *them*, you're a goner.
      No trust, no faith, no honour.

DIKAIOPOLIS.
      You've made up your mind? Decided?
310   You blame them for everything? One-sided.

CHORUS.
      What? That's the end of *you*, man.
      You claim that some of them are human?

DIKAIOPOLIS.
      Yes, some. They're not all shameless.
      Like us: not all of *us* are blameless.

CHORUS.
      My heart! It's stopped. I'm choking.
      Not shameless, *them?* You're joking.

DIKAIOPOLIS.
      I'll speak. You take this knife. Don't drop it.
      My neck – if I don't convince you, chop it.

CHORUS.
      Knives? Necks? We're talking arms and shoulders.
320   Grab gravel, men. Sling stones. Bung boulders.

DIKAIOPOLIS.
      Who fanned your flames? No, wait!
      Don't get in such a state.
      I'll explain.

CHORUS.
  Not a word.

DIKAIOPOLIS.
  It's absurd.

CHORUS.
  You'll feel pain.

DIKAIOPOLIS.
  Oh, will I? Back!
  Don't dare attack.
  You'll whinge and whine.
  It's hostage time.

  He runs inside.

CHORUS.
  What does he mean?
  It's quite obscene.
  What hostage? Where?
  In *there*?
  Our little boy?
  Our pride and joy?   330

  DIKAIOPOLIS *returns with a brazier of coals*
  and a watering-can.

DIKAIOPOLIS.
  Keep your distance. Drop
  Those stones. One brick,
  The brazier gets it.

CHORUS.
  Stop!
  I'm feeling sick.
  Those coals are friends of mine.
  You wouldn't! Swine!

DIKAIOPOLIS.
  Ah, now you're on your knees.

CHORUS.
  They're cousins, kinsmen. Please!

DIKAIOPOLIS.
   All I want to do is plead.

CHORUS.
   Oh, plead then. All you need.
   Stand up for Sparta. Speak. Defend.
340   Just don't snuff out my dear old friend.

DIKAIOPOLIS.
   No bricks, no tricks.

CHORUS.
   No jug, no mug.

DIKAIOPOLIS.
   Your cloaks are full of rubble.

CHORUS.
   We'll empty them: no trouble.
   Look, see:
   They're flying in the breeze,
   Rock-free.
   Put your water down, please.
   You're not taking a chance.
   We're clean and we'll prove it. We'll dance.

   They dance a whirling dance.

DIKAIOPOLIS.
   I thought that'd shut your row.
   Your fellow-hotheads here, they all but died,
350   They squirted me with soot, all thanks to you.
   What's made you so sour? Have you vinegar for
      blood?
   I made a fair offer. I stuck out my neck.
   I gave you the breadknife. 'I'll speak,' I said,
   'And if I don't convince you, chop away.'
   D'you think I take *pride* in suicide?

CHORUS.
   Speak, speak. Say what you feel.
360   What is this great big deal?
   We're panting to listen, we're dying to hear.
   Stick your neck out. Talk. It was your idea.

DIKAIOPOLIS.
We've got the breadboard. We've got the knife.
We've got the speaker. No need for song and
dance.
When it comes to the Spartans, I know my lines.
I know exactly what I think, what I want to say.
But I'm still not happy. *They're* the problem.   370
Those good old men,
Those simple, honest souls:
Plain-speaking, good-hearted,
Quick with applause
So long as you tell them what they want to hear –
And twice as quick with stones, when things go wrong.
I haven't forgotten that play last year,
That comedy, Aristophanes poking fun
At Kleon – and being dragged before the beak
To be slandered and slobbered and spat on,   380
Dumped on and jumped on and shat on –
For what? For nothing! What *was* that all about?
This time I'll be more careful. Take precautions.
Look before I leap. This business is serious:
I'll take it seriously. I'll dress the part.

CHORUS.
Get on with it. Stop wriggling. Start!
Who cares what you wear for the part?
Wear a top hat, a corset, wear dancing shoes –
We'll like it or hate it – just let us choose!

DIKAIOPOLIS.
I'll stiffen up the sinews, gird the soul,
And pay Euripides a social call.[3]

He knocks on EURIPIDES' *door.*

I say! Hello-oh!

KEPHISOPHON *opens the door.*

KEPHISOPHON.
What?

DIKAIOPOLIS.
    Is sir within?

KEPHISOPHON.
    Within, without. A riddle, nuncle. Hey?

DIKAIOPOLIS.
    What d'you mean, within, without?

KEPHISOPHON.
    It's simple. Look:
    His lordship's mind is floating free without,
    Gathering odelets. His body's here, within,
    Aloft, at work.

DIKAIOPOLIS (*to the audience*).
400   D'you hear that? 'Odelets'. 'Nuncle'.
    This has to be the place.

    (*to* KEPHISOPHON)

    Oi, call the boss.

KEPHISOPHON.
    He's not to be disturbéd.

DIKAIOPOLIS.
    Tough. I'm here,
    And here I stay. Make what you like of that.

    KEPHISOPHON *goes in and slams the door.*

    Ah. Knock again. Euripides! Eur-ee!
    Pray lend an ear. God knows I need one. Oo-oo!
    It's Dikaiopolis, your neighbour. Me.

    EURIPIDES *pokes his head from an upstairs window.*

EURIPIDES.
    I'm busy.

DIKAIOPOLIS.
    Use a stage effect.

EURIPIDES.
    I can't.

DIKAIOPOLIS.
  Of course you can. You always do.

EURIPIDES.
  All right.
  If it gets it over quicker. Just a mo.

  EURIPIDES *is revealed aloft, at work*[4].

DIKAIOPOLIS.
  High tragedy. So this is how it's done.   410
  Euripides.

EURIPIDES.
  What?

DIKAIOPOLIS.
  Why the rags? No cash?
  No inspiration? Sorry. Start again.
  Friend, Athenian, countryman, lend me your ears.
  No, lend me some rags. Some really tragic rags.
  I have to speak a page-long monologue.
  Persuade the Chorus. If I don't, I die.

EURIPIDES.
  I see. Something fine, but moving.
  H'm. There's this.
  I wore it as Oineus once.
  Sensational.

DIKAIOPOLIS.
  A bit too...dressy.

EURIPIDES.
  I know what you mean.   420
  There's this. I gave my Phoinix in this.

DIKAIOPOLIS.
  Some kind of revival, was it?

EURIPIDES.
  Philoktetes?

DIKAIOPOLIS.
  Too limp.

EURIPIDES.
I beg your pardon. *Limp?*

DIKAIOPOLIS.
Sore foot.

EURIPIDES.
But a great big part.

DIKAIOPOLIS.
It's not really me. But you're in the area.

EURIPIDES.
What area?

DIKAIOPOLIS.
Pathetic beggars.

EURIPIDES.
Got it!
Pathetic beggar, ragged clothes – but lines!
What lines!

DIKAIOPOLIS.
What lines?

EURIPIDES.
Persuasive lines. Knocks 'em dead each time.
No eye is dry.

DIKAIOPOLIS.
I'll take them. Whose?

EURIPIDES.
Remember *Telephos?*
The notices? Well, *this* is what I wore.

DIKAIOPOLIS.
430   Not Telephos! You'd let me borrow those?

EURIPIDES.
Of course. Slave! Give yon suppliant this.
The cloak as well. Down there, you dummy.
Underneath *The House of Atreus.*
By *Ino.*

KEPHISOPHON.
Got it.

(*to* DIKAIOPOLIS)

Here.

DIKAIOPOLIS (*peering through holes in the costume*).
O lord! O Zeus, who sees all, sees through all,
Grant me success. In holiness I beg.
Euripides, thanks. Just one more thing:
The hat. I seem to remember, he had a hat.
'I doff my hat. Scoff not. A beggar, me?   440
I am what I am, not what I seem to be.'
I know the lines. 'I may not be the part
I play; I may not play the part I be' –
That's right: we're talking comedy here. Effect.
I'm out to bamboozle those Acharnians.

EURIPIDES.
'I may not play the part I be...' Fine line.
They *all* are. Here's the hat.

DIKAIOPOLIS.
Lord Telephos thanks you.
And now, the sticking point. I need a stick.

EURIPIDES.
Take this, and leave my door undarkened.

DIKAIOPOLIS.
Woe!
Cast off, dismissed, half-dressed and propless. Oh!
Be cunning, tongue. Be bold. Be *wonderful*.   450
Euripides, I need a lampshade: straw.

EURIPIDES.
A lampshade. Wretch, why crav'st thou raffia-work?

DIKAIOPOLIS.
No craving, nuncle. It just came over me.

EURIPIDES.
You're boring. Leave my house, my green, green nest.

DIKAIOPOLIS.
> Greens! You're obsessed.
> I blame your mother's market stall.

EURIPIDES.
> Hence, hence, begone.

DIKAIOPOLIS.
> It'll cost you...
> A chip-pan, say, or a mug with a chipped little lip.

EURIPIDES.
460   Take this – and go to Hell. You hex the house.

DIKAIOPOLIS.
> You started it. There's not much more.
> Euripides, sweetie, I've *got* to have some props.
> A begging-bowl, a squeeze of sponge.

EURIPIDES.
> My stock-in-trade! I'll have nothing left.
> One bowl, one sponge. Now go!

DIKAIOPOLIS.
> Oh Eury, darling, look.
> I can't take *this* bowl. It's empty.
> A dried-up lettuce leaf? A cabbage stalk?
> You see the effect I'm after?

EURIPIDES.
470   You're stripping all my assets.

DIKAIOPOLIS.
> As if I would.
> 'Vexation rules. Our lords do hate me so.'
> Remember? Ah! There *is* just one more thing.
> Oh lovey, look, I swear this is the last.
> I'll take, and go. Your mother's leek!
> I've got to take a leek.

EURIPIDES.
> What cheek! A leek! Close up my portals, *please*.

He is removed from view.

DIKAIOPOLIS.

  God knows I tried. I'll go without a leek.   480
  Poor soul, be strong. The fight's afoot. Don't slump.
  Defending Sparta? Not a doddle. Right.
  Step forward, on your marks. The starting line.
  What, flinching? Think Euripides. Come on.
  That's it. Soul's ready. Heart, now. Don't be shy.
  Brace up. Stand tall. Quick march.
  Put your neck on the block,
  Look the world in the eye, say what you have to say.
  That's it! That's it! God, how I love that heart.

  He puts on Telephos' costume, ready for his speech.

CHORUS.

  It's a trick. It's a try-on.   490
  You're shameless. You're iron.
  You risk your neck, defy the town,
  Turn decency upside-down.
  For cheek there's none comes near you.
  Get on with it. Let's hear you.

DIKAIOPOLIS.

  First of all, gentlemen, please excuse the clothes.
  A beggar, with attitude, talks politics?
  In a comedy? I don't apologise.
  We may tell jokes, but we still know right from   500
    wrong.
  What I say may seem strange, but it's also true.
  And there's no question here of disloyalty,
  As there was last year. Slandering the state, they said,
  In front of strangers. No tourists in tonight.
  No guests. Just you and me. Athenians.
  Cream of the crop. Plus resident aliens, of course.
  As leavening. But this is private. Family talk.

  I detest the Spartans. They slashed my vines
  As well as yours. Day and night I pray for them
  To Poseidon, Earthshaker. 'Oh god,' I cry,   510
  'Make the earth move for them. Shake their
    houses down.'

But the question remains – we're all friends here –
Are they entirely to blame, for everything?
I'll tell you a story. It all begins
With a group of people here in Athens.
Not citizens, honest, decent, salt-of-the-earth,
But wrigglers, creepy-crawlies, snakes in the grass,
Apologies for human. You know the ones I mean.
And it all begins with Megara. The ally
We didn't trust, the friend we loved to hate.
'Oh look,' they'd say, 'That cardigan's Megarian.
No tax paid. Hand it over, or else I'll tell.'
Whatever they wanted, whatever you had,
520   A rabbit, a piglet, salt, garlic, figs,
'You'd better hand them over, or else I'll tell.'
Small things. Disposable. Not hard to hide.
But then some drunken idiots slipped into Megara
And kidnapped Simaitha, Queen of Tarts.
No hiding *her*. The Megarians, rubbed raw,
Retaliated: made a sortie, nabbed
A pair of toms from Athens. Local girls,
Close friends of Perikles, the Human Zeus.[5]
That's how things started. Greece uprooted. Yells
And riots. All because of puss-puss-puss.
530   His Nibs starts rumbling, roaring, belching smoke,
And finally erupts. The Megarian Decree.
Remember? The one that sounds like a nursery
    rhyme:
'They're banned. If we see them
In markets, shops or fairs,
We'll take them by the left leg
And throw them down the stairs.'
Next thing you know, the Megarians are starving,
Begging Sparta to intervene, to get it changed,
The Pussy-Decree. The Spartans asked; we said no;
They asked again; we said no
again...again...again...
Soon all you could hear was rattling shields.
540   Beg pardon? 'Fair enough.' Why fair enough?
Suppose some Spartan yob had sailed up here

And kidnapped one of those fluffy little dogs?
Would *you* have sat and smiled? Of course not.
Ships on ships, the whole armada, 'Aye aye cap'n',
Soldiers, pay-clerks, splice the mainbrace,
Swarm the walkways, stock up with flour,
With wineskins, oar-straps, buckets, jerkins,
Nets of onions, garlic, gherkins,   550
Bye-bye kisses, scraps,
Useful leather straps,
Full-fathom-five, dog-watches, bumboats,
Sou-westers, bosuns' whistles, gumboots.
You would, of course you would. That's common
    sense.
And so would Telephos. *That's* common sense.

CHORUS A.
  Common sense? You bastard! Swine!
  You wear those rags and come out here
  And accuse us? Silence! Walls have ears.

CHORUS B.
  I believe him. I think he's right.   560
  It seems fair enough to me.

CHORUS A.
  What's 'fair' got to do with it?
  He should have shut up; he didn't; he's had it.

CHORUS B.
  What are you doing? Where are you going?
  Come back. He's bigger than you are. Wait!

The fierier members of the CHORUS *hammer on*
LAMACHOS' *door.*

CHORUS A.
  Lamachos, Thunderer,
  Gorgon-glarer, cousin, help!
  Is there a general in the house?
  A major? A corporal? We're trapped.   570
  We need you now.

Enter LAMACHOS, *in full armour and carrying
a gorgon-painted shield.*

LAMACHOS.
Whence came the call to arms? Who howled for
help?
Where must I havoc wreak, where wage wild war?
Speak up! Who gasped for gorgon, screamed for
sword?

DIKAIOPOLIS.
Oh look, it's Lamachos, the one-man war.

CHORUS A.
Sir, sir, it's him, sir, telling lies.
Just ask him what he said about us all.

LAMACHOS.
You! Beggar! Stand up straight. What is all this?

DIKAIOPOLIS.
O Lamachos, O sword-lord, man of might,
I'm sorry. Beggars aren't supposed to *speak?*

LAMACHOS.
What were the actual words? Speak up, man.

DIKAIOPOLIS.
580   Ooh.
I can't remember. I've gone all wobbly: look.
Don't point that gorgon at me. Please.

LAMACHOS.
It's gone.

DIKAIOPOLIS.
Please lay it on the ground. Face down.

LAMACHOS.
It's down.

DIKAIOPOLIS.
Now lend me a feather from your helmet. Please.

LAMACHOS.
One plume. What next?

DIKAIOPOLIS.
Next hold my head. I think
I'm going to spew.

LAMACHOS.
Did you say *spew?*
That plume was plucked –

DIKAIOPOLIS.
From a Bigmouth Brag?

LAMACHOS.
For that, you die.

DIKAIOPOLIS.
Don't kill me, please.   590
Death's far too good for me. You're so severe.
What I need is foreskin-snipping. Slice; I'm braced.

LAMACHOS.
How dare you? Beggar – general? Bite your tongue!

DIKAIOPOLIS.
A beggar – me?

LAMACHOS.
Who are you? What's your name?

DIKAIOPOLIS.
Who am I? Mr Average, Man in the Street –
Or rather, thanks to this war, Man in a Mess.
What's your name, thanks to this war? Man in Clover?

LAMACHOS.
I was officially appointed –

DIKAIOPOLIS.
By a committee of cuckoos. It makes me sick
To see honest greybeards in the ranks,   600
And tailor's dummies, men like you,
Drawing wages for swanking behind the lines:
Catering designers, protocol advisers,

Accessory administrators, career consultants,
Political spin-doctors: swankers all.

LAMACHOS.
Officially appointed.

DIKAIOPOLIS.
Clones. Like you.
Every single time. How *do* you wangle it,
While men like these get nothing? Every time.

He picks individual members of the CHORUS.

Hey, Collier, you've been around. That's right.
610 So when did they last make *you* ambassador?
What? Not? He's no one's fool, works hard.
Hey, Stoker, Coker, Ash. You've been up north,
You've been to Persia? Never? Men like him,
You say, floor-sweepings, rubbish-tips?
One day they're out with the garbage,
Next on some embassy to Carthage?

LAMACHOS.
Do we have to put up with this?

DIKAIOPOLIS.
My question exactly. Do we *have* to put up with
this?

LAMACHOS.
620 A proclamation. TO WHOM IT MAY CONCERN
(ESPECIALLY SPARTA): WE, LORD LAMACHOS,
PROCLAIM UNENDING, TOTAL WAR – BY LAND,
BY SEA, BY SHIP, BY SWORD, BY ME.

He storms into his house.

DIKAIOPOLIS.
A counter-proclamation. SALE, TODAY.
ALL WELCOME. OPEN ALL HOURS. SELL,
    BROWSE OR BUY.
NO RESTRICTIONS. NO RUBBISH. NO
    LAMACHOS. FEEL FREE.

He goes into his house.

CHORUS.
He's won. We're all on his side now. United.
Aristophanes next. Be Nice to Our Author. Ready?

He's a modest man. Known for it.
Never a word of self-praise –
Until now. It's his enemies' fault –
And the hotheads who trust what they say.   630
'He's a traitor!' (you've heard them);
'Pokes fun at democracy. Slanders the state.'
Lies and rubbish! The fact is, he helps you.
You owe him. He tells you the truth,
Stops you falling for conmen and frauds
(Oh, I'm sorry: for *ministers*,
Envoys, ambassadors, giving you tongue).
'So distinguished!' – you know how it goes,
How they oil you –
'Such taste!' – it's as if you were pilchards.   640
He shows you true politics,
Shows you what life's really like
Here at home, how our allies behave –
And they swarm here to see him,
The risk-taker who Tells It Like It Is.
And it's not just in Athens. He's known
Far and wide. When this business began,
And the Spartans sent envoys to Persia,
His Highness asked only two questions.
'Who rules the sea?' (Answer: Athens.)
'Who's mocked by that poet? They'll win –
If they listen to *him*.' Don't believe me?   650
Which island did Sparta demand?
Yes, Aigina. That's right. And whose birthplace was that?
Whose home's on Aigina? That's *right*.
It's not islands they want, it's your poet.
Don't surrender him. Keep him – and listen.
His words are the truth. Nothing but –
No fawning or flattering, bribing or boasting.
Just happiness. Listen and learn!

660   Come on, Kleon! Let's fight.
        I've got justice and right.
        What have you got? You crook!
        Every trick in the book,
        Every try, every lie,
        Every smear, every tear.
        Ah, you're done for. You'll never get clear.

        Dance with me, Muse of Acharnai!
        Leap, twirl, blaze,
        Bright as the fire in the heart of the charcoal,
        Quickened by bellows,
670   Bronzing the barbecue, kissing the fish
        While the slaves mix the pickle
        And butter the bread.
        Come and dance with me! Take me! I'm yours!

        Dance.

        We senior citizens have a bone to pick.
        We fought for you at Marathon, at Salamis,
        We earned our pension rights – and was that
           enough?
        It wasn't. Our claims are contested,
        We're dragged into court, humiliated
680   By smart-arse, beardless barristers
        Who sweep us aside like fluff, like chaff.
        We thought sea-service would bolster our old age;
        Instead we stand in the dock, mumbling, toothless,
        Straining our eyes to make out what it's all about.
        Our keen young opponent, upwardly mobile,
        Grabs us and floors us and winds us,
        Nets us with word-traps, fuddles us, muddles us,
        Grandads, great-grandads, half as old as time.
        We mumble and stumble, we're guilty, we're fined,
690   We shuffle home in tears. We tell our friends,
        'I spent my coffin-money to pay that fine.'

        Justice! How *can* it be justice?
        Old, bent, grey,
        Sweated your youth away, fighting for Athens,

Fighting the Persians –
My, how they ran as you hunted them down!
Times have changed! Now it's you
Running for cover,   700
Puffing and panting. Unfair! Unfair!

Here's a case in point. Thoukydides –
No, not him, the other one, the old one,
Bent double, silver hair, yes, that one –
Gets caught up in court with that whirlwind,
That sandstorm Kephisodemos. Yes, that one.
I broke right down, I wiped away a tear, to see
Such a pitiless pensioner-pummelling.
You should have seen Thoukydides before –
Fifty years ago, he'd have stopped that storm,   710
Faced a thousand Kephisodemoses, shouted them
        down,
Battered them, buttered them, munched them for
        lunch.
We've earned a rest. Why can't you let us sleep?
Or if you can't, why not separate the courts?
Let grandads give grandads a toothless time,
Smart-arses like Y or X fight X or Y.
The pensioner punchup! The baby bout!
It's attractive. Logical. You know it makes sense.

Dance. When it ends, DIKAIOPOLIS *comes out of
his house to set up his private market.*

DIKAIOPOLIS.
The borders of my market. Here, and here.
Inside this area, anyone at all –   720
Peloponnesians, Thebans, Megarians –
Can buy and sell with me, but not with Lamachos.
These whips are the market-inspectors:
Specially selected for firmness,
Impartiality – and their winning way
With informers, sneaks and cheats.
What's next? A signpost. I've just the thing, inside.

He goes into his house. Enter the MEGARIAN,
with his DAUGHTERS.

MEGARIAN.[6]

    At last! An Athenian market, open to Megarians.
710   Am I glad to see you? Does a baby love his Mummy?
    Come here, my wee ones. Come to Daddy. There.
    We're here. It's now. It's fill-your-belly time.
    Hey, wait. Get down. There's things to think of
        first.
    So tell me. Darling wee ones, talk to Daddy. Tell.
    Would you rather starve, or be traded, here and
        now?

DAUGHTERS.

    Traded, traded.

MEGARIAN.

    I guessed. I agree. It's the only way.
    But who'll be daft enough, who'll risk the fine
    To buy you? Let's see. We need a sneaky trick.
    I know. It works back home, so why not here?
740   It's fancy-dress time. Dress as piggy-wigs.
    I'll sell a pair of piglets. Pigs in a poke.
    Her Porkiness' daughters, sow of sows. Come on.
    You can do it. D'you want to go back home, and
        starve?
    Put on the snouts. The trotters. Into the sack.
    Now, whatever happens, squeal. You're pigs,
        remember,
    Pigs for the sacrifice. I'll call him out.
    Hey, Dikaiopolis, d'you want to buy some pigs?

DIKAIOPOLIS *comes out.*

DIKAIOPOLIS.

    What's this? A Megarian?

MEGARIAN.

750   I've come to trade.

DIKAIOPOLIS.
How's business?

MEGARIAN.
There's no business.[7]

DIKAIOPOLIS.
Like show business? Sorry.
How *are* things in Megara?

MEGARIAN.
So-so.
When I left to come here to your market,
They were debating in the assembly
How long it would take to go to Hell.

DIKAIOPOLIS.
It might solve your problems.

MEGARIAN.
True.

DIKAIOPOLIS.
Talk about something else. The price of corn.

MEGARIAN.
Sky-high.

DIKAIOPOLIS.
What have you brought me? Salt?

MEGARIAN.
You own our salt.   760

DIKAIOPOLIS.
Garlic?

MEGARIAN.
You're joking. We plant it each autumn,
You invade each spring and trample it.

DIKAIOPOLIS.
Well, what then?

MEGARIAN.
Pigs, for sticking.

DIKAIOPOLIS.
> Now you're talking. Where?

MEGARIAN.
> In here. Top quality.

DIKAIOPOLIS.
> What's this, by god?

MEGARIAN.
> A pig, by god.

DIKAIOPOLIS.
> What kind?

MEGARIAN.
> Megarian.

DIKAIOPOLIS.
> It doesn't feel like pig.

MEGARIAN.
770   Oh, charming! 'Doesn't feel like pig'!
> Of course it's pig. I bet you a bag of salt
> That's pig. 'Doesn't feel like pig'!

DIKAIOPOLIS.
> This belongs to a human.

MEGARIAN.
> Of course. It's mine.
> Whose d'you think it is? Stop messing. Look,
> D'you want to hear them squealing?

DIKAIOPOLIS.
> Wouldn't mind.

MEGARIAN.
> Squeal, pig. Squeal, piggy-wiggy, squeal.
> D'you want to go home again, empty? Squeal!

DAUGHTERS.
780   Oink oink.

MEGARIAN.
> Pig or not pig?

DIKAIOPOLIS.
  It sounds like pig.
  But what's it feel like? Flat.

MEGARIAN.
  Give it five years,
  It'll round right out, I promise you.

DIKAIOPOLIS.
  Not ready for sticking.

MEGARIAN.
  Beg pardon?

DIKAIOPOLIS.
  No tail.

MEGARIAN.
  It's far too young for tail. But feed it up
  To porkerhood, you'll see: plump, wiggly, pink.
  If it's pig you want, this is the pig for you.

DIKAIOPOLIS.
  What about this one? It feels very similar.

MEGARIAN.
  Same litter. Same parents. Just let it grow,   790
  Let it bristle, you'll be queuing up
  To sacrifice it to the god of love.

DIKAIOPOLIS.
  Who sacrifices pigs to the god of love?

MEGARIAN.
  Just sharpen your spit, and wait and see.

DIKAIOPOLIS.
  Are they weaned? Will they eat without their
    mother?

MEGARIAN.
  Poseidon, yes. Without their father, too.

DIKAIOPOLIS.
  What do they fancy?

MEGARIAN.
Whatever you give 'em.
Ask them yourself.

DIKAIOPOLIS.
Piggy-piggy-piggy.

FIRST DAUGHTER.
800   Oink.

DIKAIOPOLIS.
Can you cope with carrot?

FIRST DAUGHTER.
Oink oink.

DIKAIOPOLIS.
D'you fancy figs?[8]

FIRST DAUGHTER.
Oink oink oink.

DIKAIOPOLIS.
What about your sister?
Does little piggy-wig want figgy-wig?

SECOND DAUGHTER.
Oink oink oink oink.

DIKAIOPOLIS.
Sounds like a run on figs.
Fetch figs, and feed the pigs.

XANTHIAS *does so*.

I wonder if they'll like them. Wow! They do.
I've never seen such action in the sack.

MEGARIAN.
810   *I've* never seen such figs. Leave some for me!

DIKAIOPOLIS.
What a pair! What a credit to their parents!
I'll buy them both. What will you take for them?

MEGARIAN.
For the eldest, a bundle of garlic.
For the youngest, a bag of salt.

DIKAIOPOLIS.
It's a bargain.
Wait here.

He goes into his house.

MEGARIAN.
It worked! Who's next, I wonder?
How much for the wife? For Ma-in-law?

Enter NIKARCHOS.

NIKARCHOS.
You.
State your business.

MEGARIAN.
Pig-selling. From Megara.

NIKARCHOS.
I thought as much. I confiscate those pigs.
You're under arrest.

MEGARIAN.
Oh, here we go again.   820
Not today, not now. We've got your type at home.

NIKARCHOS.
Importing enemy pigs! Put down that sack.

MEGARIAN.
Dikaiopolis! I'm being depigged.

DIKAIOPOLIS *comes out.*

DIKAIOPOLIS.
Who by? Who's pinching those porkers?
My market inspectors want words with you.

He threatens NIKARCHOS *with the whips.*

Identification? Warrant? Flash 'em, fast!

NIKARCHOS.
  I'm a patriot. Doing my duty.

DIKAIOPOLIS.
  Fine.
  Now, vanish! Do it somewhere else.

  He drives him out.

MEGARIAN.
  Are things as bad as that in Athens too?

DIKAIOPOLIS.
830 We manage. Here: your garlic, your bag of salt.
  Leave me the pigs. Thanks. Have a nice day, now.

MEGARIAN.
  Me? You're joking.

DIKAIOPOLIS.
  I do apologise.

MEGARIAN.
  Poor little piggy-wigs. You're on your own.
  Eat what you can, as often as you can.

  Exit. DIKAIOPOLIS *takes the* DAUGHTERS *inside.*

CHORUS.
  He's doing well. He's a happy man.
  His plan
  Is quite simple: to buy and to sell
  And to send secret policemen to Hell.
840 Ktesias, for one –
  He can holler and run!

  No sneaks, no swine, no scum;
  No Smelly-Bum,
  No Great-Big-Tum:
  They just can't come.

  You won't see Kratinos here, that skunk,
  That punk,
  That disaster, that social disease
  With his underarm odour – no, *please!* –

Not that festering fink   850
With his cesspit-like stink.

Hyperbolos, don't come.
You're dim, you're dumb,
You bore us numb;
You've had it, chum.

Enter THEBAN, *preceded by* BAGPIPERS *and followed
by* ISMENIAS, *loaded with market produce.*

THEBAN.[6]
  By Herakles, I think I've cricked my back.   860
  Ismenias, put down that lettuce. Help me!
  You lads, don't think you came all the way from Thebes
  For nothing. Give us a chorus of 'The Dog's Behind'.

  Bagpipe music. Enter DIKAIOPOLIS.

DIKAIOPOLIS.
  Fooagh. Stop. Shoo.
  It's a bee-swarm. A wasps' nest.
  You're worse than Chairis. Stop!

  Silence.

THEBAN.
  Thanks, pal. I was getting desperate.
  They've followed me all the way from Thebes,
  Wheezing and whistling. They've wrecked my lettuce.
  Anyhow, pal, this is your lucky day.   870
  I've brought you poultry: all you'll ever need.

DIKAIOPOLIS.
  What sort of poultry?

THEBAN.
  Theban poultry. Poultry in motion. *And –*
  D'you feel the need for wicks at all?
  Rush matting? Firewood? Mint?

DIKAIOPOLIS.
  Poultry.

THEBAN.
  Right.
  I've ducks, quails, pigeons, blackbirds, rooks –

DIKAIOPOLIS.
  That's fowl.

THEBAN.
  The foulest you'll find. And as well as fowl
  I've foxes, hedgehogs, weasels, bats, moles, voles;
880 I've badgers, polecats, otters, beavers, eels –

DIKAIOPOLIS.
  Did you say eels? My favourite food! Oh please,
  Bring out your eels, let me feel those eels.

  The THEBAN *rummages in one of* ISMENIAS' *fish-baskets.*

THEBAN.
  Come out here, eel, come out. Dear daughter of
  The limpid lake, come out and say hello.

  He hands DIKAIOPOLIS *an eel.*

DIKAIOPOLIS.
  You're beautiful. How long we've longed for you,
  We lovers of fine comedy, fine fish.
  Xanthias, ho! My stove, my bellows bring.
  She's here, the longed-for one, she's here at last.
890 For seven eelless years we've yearned for her.
  My little ones, speak welcome. Look, and smile.
  I'll stir the fire. I'll make her welcome warm.
  Eel stew, methinks. With beetroot gravy. Yum.

THEBAN.
  Ahem. You want her, do you, want to trade?

DIKAIOPOLIS.
  I'll take her on her own, or take the lot.
  Lock, stock and barrel. It's up to you.

THEBAN.
In that case, take the lot.

DIKAIOPOLIS.
Good. Name your price.
Or take some local produce. Tit for tat.

THEBAN.
What local produce? Something new to Thebes.   900

DIKAIOPOLIS.
Sardines? A Grecian urn?

THEBAN.
We're up to here with urns.
We're sick of sardines. Try something else.
Something where you've a glut, and we've got none.

DIKAIOPOLIS.
A secret policeman? We've got a glut of those.
Ready wrapped?

THEBAN.
I like it. I'll put him on show,
Like a monkey in a cage.
He'll take particulars from passers-by.
I'll charge. I'll make my fortune.

DIKAIOPOLIS.
Here's one, now.

THEBAN.
Bit small.

DIKAIOPOLIS.
But every inch a bastard.

Enter NIKARCHOS.

NIKARCHOS.
Whose goods are these?

THEBAN.
They're mine. From Thebes.   910

NIKARCHOS.
They're confiscated. Prohibited imports.
War-materials.

THEBAN.
You're joking. They're poultry.

NIKARCHOS.
You're under arrest.

THEBAN.
What for?

NIKARCHOS.
These, for a start.
You've imported terrorist lampwicks.

THEBAN.
How can lampwicks be terrorist?

NIKARCHOS.
Incendiary devices. In a shipyard – whoosh!

DIKAIOPOLIS.
A lampwick. A shipyard. Whoosh?

NIKARCHOS.
No question.

DIKAIOPOLIS.
How?

NIKARCHOS.
920   Your Theban terrorist attaches it
To a cockroach, lights it, floats it down the drain
To the nearest shipyard. North wind. Whoosh!
Our entire armada, up in smoke.

DIKAIOPOLIS.
Because of a wick and a cockroach?

NIKARCHOS.
That's my case.

DIKAIOPOLIS.
Grab him. Gag him. Bring some string.

I'll pack him. Fragile. This way up.
Like a great big pot.

He starts trussing and packing NIKARCHOS.

CHORUS.
Pull harder. Heave.
For the customer's sake,   930
Truss the bastard tight.
He mustn't break.

DIKAIOPOLIS.
I know what I'm doing.
He's safely packed.
Just a minute! Here!
This pot sounds cracked.

He knocks NIKARCHOS. NIKARCHOS *howls.*

CHORUS.
What's it good for?

DIKAIOPOLIS.
Confusion, lies,
Long lawsuits, grief,
Pain, tears and sighs
Without relief.

CHORUS.
Such wails! Such moans!   940
Such groans and howls!
Who wants a pot
That yaps and yowls?

DIKAIOPOLIS.
It's solid, hard,
The best in town.
Won't even break
Hung upside-down.

CHORUS.
There: packed and ready.

THEBAN.
Mine! I'm made!

CHORUS.
If he gives you pain
950   Let him ply his trade
Right down the drain.

DIKAIOPOLIS.
The bastard's ready. Tied, trussed and delivered.
He's all yours, pal. Your little crock of gold.

THEBAN.
Bend down, Ismenias. Get your shoulder under.

DIKAIOPOLIS.
Don't drop him. He may be scum,
But he's a nice little nest-egg too. And if this one
    suits,
Come back for more. We've still got glut.

Exeunt THEBAN *and entourage, with the trussed*
NIKARCHOS. *Enter* AIDE DE CAMP.

AIDE DE CAMP.
Dikaiopolis.

DIKAIOPOLIS.
What a fright you gave me. What?

AIDE DE CAMP.
His Magnificence bestows on you four drachs.
The commissariat requires: roast thrush, one
960   drach,
For Glug-Glug Day, and three drachs' worth of eel.

DIKAIOPOLIS.
Which Magnificence is this requireth eel?

AIDE DE CAMP.
His Hugeness, His Fierceness, Gorgon-lord,
Master of Havoc, Prince of the Purple Plume.

DIKAIOPOLIS.

Oh, Lamachos. No thrushes today. No chance.
His Hugeness, eels? His plume's not worth sardines.
Tell him my market inspectors say, 'Get stuffed.'
I'm going in. I wing it, borne on high
By a flutter of feathered friends. Bye-bye.   970

He goes in, carrying all the birds. Exit
AIDE DE CAMP.

CHORUS.

A man of talent, friends. A bulging brain.
He risked his neck, he won,
And now he's in clover, as right as rain.

No more parties for War,
No more marching-songs,
Guzzling or boozing – he's banned.   980
He's a loudmouth, a drunk;
He comes swaggering in,
Shouting, quarrelling, banging the table –
And when you say, 'Drink this, for friendship'
He burns all your vine-poles
And tramples your grapes.

Our hero chanced his arm, and passed the test.
It's celebration time.

A cloud of feathers is thrown out from
DIKAIOPOLIS' *house.*

He's plucky. He's lucky. He's feathering his nest.

Come and live with me, Peace,   990
Little sister of Friendship and Quiet.
Come down; make me happy.
What can I offer you,
Old as I am? I've a vine-branch that's sappy,
Figs bursting with juice. You'll enjoy it!
Fertility dances,
The rustle of spring.

Dance. When it ends, enter TOWN CRIER.

TOWN CRIER.
1000   Hear this. By order. It's Glug-Glug Day.
    At the sound of the trumpet, throughout the land,
    Drink up. It's a glug-glug race. First prize:
    A skin of wine as fat as Ktesiphon.

DIKAIOPOLIS *bustles out, organising his family
and household.*

DIKAIOPOLIS.
    You heard him. Get a move on. Over here.
    Roast, grill, fry, boil, simmer, stew.
    See to the rabbits. The party-crowns!
    Pass over those skewers. I'll start the thrush kebab.

CHORUS.
    What style! What art!
1010   What panache! What ease!

DIKAIOPOLIS.
    Just wait till I start
    Spit-roasting these.

CHORUS.
    What skill!

DIKAIOPOLIS.
    The grill.

CHORUS.
    When you're grilling
    You're thrilling.
    What grace!
    You're ace.

Enter YOKEL, *in deep mourning.*

YOKEL.
    Oo-ah. Ahaah.

DIKAIOPOLIS.
    Who's this?

YOKEL.
  A poor old man.

DIKAIOPOLIS.
  Not here. Not now.

YOKEL.
  They say you've made some kind of private peace.   1020
  Be neighbourly. Pour me a year or two...or five...

DIKAIOPOLIS.
  What's wrong with you?

YOKEL.
  What's right?
  I'm ruined. They took away Daisy, Buttercup.
  My cows.

DIKAIOPOLIS.
  Who did?

YOKEL.
  The Thebans.

DIKAIOPOLIS.
  That's why you're dressed like that?

YOKEL.
  I'm dressed like this for Daisy, for Buttercup.
  For how they used to keep me. Rolling.

DIKAIOPOLIS.
  So what comes next?

YOKEL.
  I've cried my eyes out for them.
  Daisy! Buttercup! Ahaah! Look, neighbour,
  Can't you see your way...a smear of peace, here, here,
  To help me see my way...?

DIKAIOPOLIS.
  I'm not an optician.   1030

YOKEL.
  I just want Daisy, Buttercup. Oh please!

DIKAIOPOLIS.
>You want the slaughterhouse. Down there.

YOKEL.
>One drop!
>A droplet. I've brought a bottle. Drop!

DIKAIOPOLIS.
>Not even a driplet. Don't do that! Go away!

YOKEL.
>Oh Daisy. Buttercup. Ahaah. Ahaah.

Exit.

CHORUS.
>What nerve! What style!
>What finesse! What zest!
>He won't share his pile
>With just any old pest.

DIKAIOPOLIS.
1040   Reveal
>The eel.

CHORUS.
>What feeling!
>I'm reeling.
>You make
>Me quake.

DIKAIOPOLIS.
>Don't just brown the outside. Cook it through and
>through.

Enter BEST MAN *and* BRIDESMAID.

BEST MAN.
>Dikaiopolis.

DIKAIOPOLIS.
>What now?

BEST MAN.
  I'm from the wedding up the road. The groom
  Sends all best wishes, and this sausage roll.

DIKAIOPOLIS.
  Whoever he is, how kind.   1050

BEST MAN.
  He asks you to eat his health,
  And in return, to send him a drop of peace.
  He's just been called up; he's better things to do;
  Your peace could see to that. In this cup, here.

DIKAIOPOLIS.
  Take back your sausage roll! A drop of peace?
  I wouldn't part – just a minute. Who's this?

BEST MAN.
  Chief bridesmaid. Asking a favour. From the bride.
  She'll whisper it herself.

DIKAIOPOLIS.
  Well? Don't be shy.

  The BRIDESMAID *whispers.*

  Good grief! What a thing to ask! As long as *that?*   1060
  Bring out the treaty. How can I refuse?
  She's a woman; she's hardly to blame for war.
  You've got the bottle there? Good. Hold it out.
  And here's the prescription. Tell her every word.
  'Three times a day, or whenever the warcry sounds,
  Whichever is more frequent. Rub well in.'

  Exeunt BEST MAN *and* BRIDESMAID.

  Take the treaty inside. Bring a skin of wine.
  It's Glug-Glug Day. I ought to try my luck.

CHORUS.
  There's someone coming. Knotted eyebrows.
  It has to be important. Major news.   1070

  Enter TOWN CRIER.

TOWN CRIER.
Emergency! Big fight! Yoh Lamachos!

LAMACHOS *comes out.*

LAMACHOS.
Hahaah! Who came? Who called? Who hailed my
house?

TOWN CRIER.
An urgent signal, sir, from G.H.Q.
TO LAMACHOS, PRIORITY, ACTION THIS DAY
DROP EVERYTHING. DON ARMOUR.
SHOULDER SHIELD.
PATROL ALL PEAKS. GUARD GLACIERS.
MESSAGE ENDS.
It's because of Glug-Glug Day. Some Theban thugs
Are planning plunder. They've had intelligence.

LAMACHOS.
Intelligence? You're joking. From G.H.Q.?
My Splendour had other plans for Glug-Glug Day.

DIKAIOPOLIS.
1080 'My Splendour had Other Plans.' Brace up, man,
brace.

LAMACHOS.
How dare you mock me, midget? Stand and fight.

DIKAIOPOLIS.
Watch out. This loaf is lethal. Make my day.

LAMACHOS.
A-ee!
What tiresome tidings he tramped up here to tell.

DIKAIOPOLIS.
A-ee! I think he's some for me as well.

TOWN CRIER.
Dikaiopolis.

DIKAIOPOLIS.
What?

TOWN CRIER.
An urgent message.
TO DIKAIOPOLIS. PERSONAL. ACTION THIS DAY.
DROP EVERYTHING. BRING PLATE AND SPOON
    AND COME
TO GLUG-GLUG FEAST. MESSAGE ENDS. R.S.V.P.
They're waiting. In the green room.[9] Now.
You're all they need. Everything else is ready:
Sofas, tables, cushions, rugs,   1090
Wine-jars, barrels, bottles, jugs,
Cakes, buns, biscuits, shortbread, tarts,
Did I mention...tarts?
D'you get my meaning...tarts?
Just as soon as you get there, the party starts.

Exit.

LAMACHOS.
A-oh-ho-ho.

DIKAIOPOLIS.
Stop moaning. You made *your* bed, and I made mine.
Bring the meat-tray, Xanthias. Lock up inside.

SLAVES *prepare* DIKAIOPOLIS *and* LAMACHOS *for
departure.*

LAMACHOS.
That man! My field-pack, now.

DIKAIOPOLIS.
That man! My meal-pack. Wow!

LAMACHOS.
Salt fish. Dried onions. Quick.

DIKAIOPOLIS.
Dried onions make me sick.   1100

LAMACHOS.
An inch of stale salami.

DIKAIOPOLIS.
No thanks. D'you think I'm barmy?

LAMACHOS.
My epaulettes. My baton.

DIKAIOPOLIS.
That pigeon pie. Put that on.

LAMACHOS.
How wondrous white these buttons gleam.

DIKAIOPOLIS.
How ready to bite these drumsticks seem.

LAMACHOS.
You there. Stop fooling.

DIKAIOPOLIS.
If *you* stop drooling.

LAMACHOS.
Fetch forth our helmet crest.

DIKAIOPOLIS.
1110   Pâté de chicken breast.

LAMACHOS.
Ye gods! Moths! Look: my plume!

DIKAIOPOLIS.
Hare soup! I hope I've room.

LAMACHOS.
Don't speak to me. Behave.

DIKAIOPOLIS.
I'm talking to my slave.

(*to* XANTHIAS)

Well, *I* can't answer. *Ask* him. Now. Defer.

(*to* LAMACHOS)

Lord, crumbs or crumpet, which do *you* prefer?

LAMACHOS.
Enough!

DIKAIOPOLIS.
  Cream puff?

  (*to* XANTHIAS)

  He'll risk it.
  He'll take the biscuit.

LAMACHOS.
  Unhook and bring to me my spear.

DIKAIOPOLIS.
  Unhook and bring my sausage here.

LAMACHOS.
  With this I'll win.   1120

DIKAIOPOLIS.
  What crunchy skin.

LAMACHOS.
  My shield-stand.

DIKAIOPOLIS.
  My doggy-bag.

LAMACHOS.
  Now, my shield!
  My gorgon stands revealed.

DIKAIOPOLIS.
  My cheesecake! What a beauty!
  So creamy, fresh and fruity.

LAMACHOS.
  Impertinence!

DIKAIOPOLIS.
  But certain sense.

LAMACHOS.
  Buff up the buckler, slave. Ha! What see I?
  I see an old fool tried for cowardice.

DIKAIOPOLIS.
1130   Oil well the cake-stand, slave. Ha! What see I?
   While Lamachos weeps, an old fool takes the piss.

LAMACHOS.
   My breastplate.

DIKAIOPOLIS.
   My dinnerplate.

LAMACHOS.
   For defeating.

DIKAIOPOLIS.
   For eating.

LAMACHOS.
   My bedroll. My big, big, boot.

DIKAIOPOLIS.
   My breadroll. My dinner-suit.

LAMACHOS.
1140   Bags, HUP. By the left, quick – Fwah!
   It's cold. Oh no! Not snow!

DIKAIOPOLIS.
   Food-baskets, HUP! By the left, quick MUNCH.
   We'll be just in time for lunch.

   Exeunt.

CHORUS.
   Two processions,
   Two professions.
   One to shiver
   And shudder
   In the snow, on guard.
   One to snuggle
   And cuddle
   With a girl. It's hard.
   First the banquet, then the beauty.
   Someone has to. Public duty.

Ladies and gentlemen, an interlude.[10]   1150
Subject, Antimachos. What do you mean,
Antimachos Who? Old Spitface.
Our former backer. Our one-time angel. The man
With the petrified purse-strings,
Who takes you to dinner and leaves you to pay.

Zeus, stop him.
A sizzling dish of cuttlefish;
He comes in late; he salivates;
He sits; he grabs; he's cursed.
My doggy nabbed it first.   1160
That's bad. How sad.
My doggy nabbed it first.

Zeus, bop him.
It's night; he's tight; he's in a fight;
He's all alone; he grabs a stone –
No, that's absurd, a turd –   1170
And hits Kratinos by mistake.
Oh dear. Don't jeer.
Kratinos, by mistake.

Enter LAMACHOS' AIDE DE CAMP.

AIDE DE CAMP.
Woe, woe. Warm water well.
Fetch lint, a splint.
His Fierceness leapt a fence, a fearsome fence,
And such is fate, he fell.
Sprained ankle. Pain!
He tried to stand up; he knocked his nut   1180
On a signpost, and smashed his shield.
He saw that gorgon go. He gasped, he gulped,
He plucked his plume, shed manly tears.
'Dear daylight, Sun – well, nightlight, Moon'
(He cried), 'I die. So young! So soon!'
So saying, on he staggered, down a drain,
Then up, proud prince, impervious to pain,

He broke those bastards, made them fear his spear.
Dread, direful deeds... Oops, open up! He's here.

Enter LAMACHOS, *supported by two* ORDERLIES.

LAMACHOS.
1190   Atta-ta-ee.
        What fate. What fearful, frightful fate.
        I'm speared, I'm spiked.
        They've done for me.
        Thank the gods Dikaiopolis
        Isn't here to see.

Enter DIKAIOPOLIS, *supported by two* DANCING-
GIRLS.

DIKAIOPOLIS.
        Wee-hee-hee.
        What breasts. What bouncy, bobbly breasts.
1200   Hey, kiss me, pet.
        What lips, what eyes.
        At the Glug-Glug Feast
        I won first prize.

LAMACHOS.
        Ee-ee, oh-oh,
        What piercing pain.

DIKAIOPOLIS.
        Hee-hee, ho-ho,
        It's him again.

LAMACHOS.
        Ow-ooh.

DIKAIOPOLIS.
        Another kiss?

LAMACHOS.
        Ah-haah.

DIKAIOPOLIS.
        Like this?

LAMACHOS.
Oh hateful fate.   1210

DIKAIOPOLIS.
Was that a moan?

LAMACHOS.
Oh no! My toe!

DIKAIOPOLIS.
Was that a groan?

LAMACHOS.
My ankle's wrecked.
Massage my knees.

DIKAIOPOLIS.
I'm half-erect.
Massage me, please.

LAMACHOS.
I'm dizzy! See! I whirl!
I curse my luck.

DIKAIOPOLIS.
We're busy: me and this girl.   1220
We're going to...bed.

LAMACHOS.
Heal me, oh heal me well.
I'm fading fast.

DIKAIOPOLIS.
Feel me, oh feel me swell.
First prize, at last.

LAMACHOS (*as he is carried inside*).
My marrow hurts! They speared me, here.

DIKAIOPOLIS.
I drained the wineskin. Oh, my dear!

SLAVES *bring in an enormous, phallic wineskin.*

CHORUS.
Here comes the next one. Drink this down!

DIKAIOPOLIS.
No problem. Where's my victor's crown?

CHORUS.
Procession time. Get up.

They lift him shoulder-high.

1230   Now, fill your cup.

DIKAIOPOLIS.
I'll lead the way.
Oh happy day.

CHORUS.
He'll lead the way.
Oh happy, happy day.

Exeunt in procession.

KNIGHTS

Characters

DEMOSTHENES
NIKIAS
AGORAKRITOS
PAPHLAGON
DEMOS

Silent parts:

DECKCHAIR ATTENDANT
TWO GORGEOUS GIRLS
SLAVES

CHORUS OF KNIGHTS

An open space, in front of DEMOS' *house. Clatter and howling from inside the house. The door is opened, and* DEMOSTHENES *and* NIKIAS *are flung out head over heels.*

DEMOSTHENES.
Ow! Ooh! Ouch!
Damn! Damn! Damn that new slave, that Paphlagon.
Him and his tricks. Damn him, damn him to hell.
Ever since he arrived, he's brought nothing
But trouble and beatings for all the rest of us.

NIKIAS.
Ow! That Paphlagon. Oh! That lying swine.

DEMOSTHENES.
There, there. Where does it hurt?

NIKIAS.
Everywhere. Same as you.

DEMOSTHENES.
There's only one thing for it. A little duet.
You know the one I mean. Are you ready?

BOTH.
Mooh, mooh, moo-mooh, mooh, moo-mooh, moo-
    mooh, moo-mooh...   10

DEMOSTHENES.
Ah, that's no good. There must be some other way.

NIKIAS.
Well?

DEMOSTHENES.
Well, what?

NIKIAS.
I'm listening.

DEMOSTHENES.
After you.

NIKIAS.
It was your idea.

DEMOSTHENES.
I've *no* idea.

NIKIAS.
Speak now, or forever hold your peace.

DEMOSTHENES.
Eh?

NIKIAS.
To be, or not to be, that is the question.

DEMOSTHENES.
No it bloody isn't. What good will that do?
20   Oh, I don't know...can you spare me the next dance?

NIKIAS.
No, no, no, no. Just a minute. Say 'purr'.

DEMOSTHENES.
All right. 'Purr'.

NIKIAS.
Good. Now 'Wheel-scar'.

DEMOSTHENES.
Eh?

NIKIAS.
'Wheel-scar'.

DEMOSTHENES.
'Wheel-scar'.

NIKIAS.
Very good. Now try them both together,
One after the other, faster and faster,
Like you do when you're jerking off.

DEMOSTHENES.
Purr. Wheel-scar. Purr. Wheel-scar. Purr.
Wheel-scar-purr. Wheelscarpurr...wheelscarpurr...
WE'LL SCARPER!

NIKIAS.
Good idea?

DEMOSTHENES.
Oh yes. Except for the wine.

NIKIAS.
  What wine?

DEMOSTHENES.
  My whine, when they catch us and beat us up.

NIKIAS.
  There's only one thing for it, then. Your knees.

DEMOSTHENES.
  Pardon?

NIKIAS.
  Get down on your knees, and pray.   30

DEMOSTHENES.
  You don't mean you still believe in the gods?

NIKIAS.
  Of course.

DEMOSTHENES.
  And how d'you know the gods exist?

NIKIAS.
  Simple: just look at the way they're treating me.

DEMOSTHENES.
  Oh, very clever. There must be some other way.
  I know. I'll put it to the audience.

NIKIAS.
  Not bad...if you're sure they're on our side.
  What do they think of it so far? Ask and see.

DEMOSTHENES.
  All right. I'm ready. Ladies and gentlemen,   40
  Our master's called Demos (as in Demo-cracy).
  A white-haired old gentleman: thick, cross, deaf...
  You know the sort. Last month, at the auction,
  He bought a new slave. A tanner, called Kle –
  Er, Paphlagon. A low-down, lying swine...
  Gives worms a bad name. He very soon found out
  How to handle Demos (The People. Our master.)
  He took him in hand, like a worn-out shoe,

And oiled him and soaked him and softened him up.
50   You know the technique. 'Oh Demos, oh sir,
Don't tire yourself out. Judge one little case,
Then come home to a bath and a good dinner.
It's your favourite. Shall I hold the spoon?'
The old man sits there and grins, and Paphlagon
Grabs someone else's cooking and serves it up
Himself. The other day I'd made a stew,
A lovely hash of Spartans at Pylos –
And he rushed in, snatched it, and dished it up...
My hash, not his. We can't get near the Boss:
60   *He's* always there, waiting at table,
Swatting the opposition with a whip, like flies.
And that's not all. The old man's superstitious,
Hooked on horoscopes. So what does our friend do?
He gets him glassy-eyed on oracles
And fills him with fairy-tales about the staff.
We get a whipping, and Paphlagon goes round
The others with a smile and a collecting-box.
Hush money. Insurance. Protection fund.
'You saw the beating Hylas got? All thanks
To me. You know what to do, or you'll be next.'
We know what to do. We pay. Because if we don't,
70   The old man'll beat us till we shit an octopus.

(*to* NIKIAS)

So think of something quick. This is no joke.

NIKIAS.
I've told you. Purr. Wheel-scar. It's the only way.

DEMOSTHENES.
But where can we go, away from Paphlagon?
He's everywhere. One foot here in Athens
Trampling the Assembly; a thumb on Thebes,
A finger in Phigaleia, a behind as wide
As the Saronic Gulf; wherever you go
His beady eyes are watching, his hands held out.

NIKIAS.

There's only one safe place. The grave.　　　　80

DEMOSTHENES.

H'm.

It would have to be a proper death, a hero's death.

NIKIAS.

Suppose we take poison, like Themistokles?

A gallon of bull's blood – that did for him.

DEMOSTHENES.

Die of drink, eh? That sounds a good idea.

But not bull's blood. Wine's good enough for
　　me.

NIKIAS.

Wine! Wine! That's all you ever think about.

We've got to *think*. There isn't time for wine.

DEMOSTHENES.

No time for wine? What are you, some kind of freak?

Teetotal? Water on the brain? No time for *wine*?　　90

Drinking *is* thinking – can't you see? Drink makes

Us rich, brave, happy, nice to our friends...

Oh, bring me some wine. *I'll* show you how to think.

NIKIAS.

I don't see how it helps if you get drunk.

DEMOSTHENES.

But I do. Get the wine.

NIKIAS *goes inside.*

I'll sit down here,

Fill up with wine, and sprinkle all the world

With schemes and plans and showers of bright ideas. 100

NIKIAS *comes back with wine.*

NIKIAS.

Our luck was in for once. I pinched the wine

And no one saw me.

DEMOSTHENES.
What's Paphlagon doing?

NIKIAS.
That bastard! He traded his extortion fund
For salted nuts. Now he's drunk as a lord,
Snoring, flat on his back on a pile of hides.

DEMOSTHENES.
Pour me some wine, then. A big one, go on:
I want to drink a toast.

NIKIAS.
To the god of luck?

DEMOSTHENES.
To the god in the jug.

He drinks.

Hey! I've got it!
I knew the answer was here inside this jug.

NIKIAS.
What answer?

DEMOSTHENES.
Go inside, while Paphlagon's asleep,
110   And...pinch his oracles.

NIKIAS.
Eh?

DEMOSTHENES.
Oracles...prophecies...horoscopes. Bring them
   here.

NIKIAS.
All right. But if that's what you call a good idea...

He goes in.

DEMOSTHENES.
Now, do I want another? Yes, I do.
If you want fountains of ideas, you have
To keep the cistern full.

He drinks. NIKIAS *comes back, with a roll of parchment.*

NIKIAS.
Look: the oracles.
His pride and joy. He was snoring and farting,
Making such a row, he didn't hear a thing.

DEMOSTHENES.
Good. Give them to me. I'll have a quick look.
Oh, and pour me a drink. Now, what does it say...?
Heavens! No, really? Phew! Give me another drink.   120

NIKIAS.
Here. What does it say?

DEMOSTHENES.
Bottoms up.

NIKIAS.
Bottoms up?
Does it really say 'Bottoms up' in there?

DEMOSTHENES (*reading*).
Oh, Bakis!

NIKIAS.
Eh?

DEMOSTHENES (*to him*).
Fill it up again.

NIKIAS.
Oh.
That's who Bakis is: one of your drunken friends.

DEMOSTHENES.
No, no. Bakis the prophet. No wonder
That bastard Paphlagon kept *this* to himself.
It's all about *him*.

NIKIAS.
About Paphlagon?

DEMOSTHENES.
The Downfall of Paphlagon. It's all in here.

NIKIAS.
When? How? What does it say?

DEMOSTHENES.
It's down here. Look:
130   A LIST OF ALL THE BOSSES OF THE STATE.
First, a rope-knotter[11].

NIKIAS.
A rope-knotter. H'm. Go on.

DEMOSTHENES.
Next, a sheep-seller.

NIKIAS.
A sheep-seller. Still a bit woolly.
What happens to him?

DEMOSTHENES.
He goes on being Big Boss
Till an even filthier crook turns up
And throws him out. And it says here, the next
Is our Paphlagon. Look: NEXT, THIRD IN LINE,
A LEATHER-SELLER WITH A GREAT BIG
    MOUTH
AND ITCHY FINGERS.

NIKIAS.
That's really what it says?
The leather-seller throws the sheep-seller out?

DEMOSTHENES.
That's right.

NIKIAS.
140   Oh golly! We need one seller more.

DEMOSTHENES.
And we've got one. Groo! What a funny trade.

NIKIAS.
What does he do?

DEMOSTHENES.
Guess.

NIKIAS.
  Tell me, for heaven's sake.

DEMOSTHENES.
  Listen, then. A DEALER IN GUTS AND TRIPE
  COMES NEXT, AND THROWS THE LEATHER-
    SELLER OUT.

NIKIAS.
  A sausage-seller? What a lovely job.
  Where will we find one?

DEMOSTHENES.
  We'll have to go and look.

NIKIAS.
  No, it's all right: there's one coming now. There.
  Isn't that lucky?

  Enter AGORAKRITOS.

DEMOSTHENES.
  O welcome, welcome
  Sausage-seller! Noblest of mortals...saviour...
  Reveal yourself at last. Oh, walk this way.

AGORAKRITOS.
  What is it? What d'you want?

DEMOSTHENES.
  Come over here,   150
  And let me tell you your fantastic luck.

NIKIAS.
  Get him to put his tray down, and show him
  The oracle. I've got to see to Paphlagon.

  He goes in[12].

DEMOSTHENES (*to* AGORAKRITOS).
  Come here. That's right. Now put your tray down here.

  AGORAKRITOS *unslings his tray, and bends to put
  it on the ground.* DEMOSTHENES *pushes him headlong.*

That's right. Give Mother Earth a great big kiss.

AGORAKRITOS.
What's the big idea?

DEMOSTHENES.
I'm telling your fortune, mate.
Today, nobody; tomorrow, the world.
Big Boss of Athens. Highest of the High.

AGORAKRITOS.
160   Look, mate, I haven't time for games.
I've sausages to sell and tripe to wash.

DEMOSTHENES.
Tripe? *Tripe?* Look out there.
D'you see them? The people.
Rows and rows of them.

AGORAKRITOS.
I see them. What of it?

DEMOSTHENES.
They're yours, all yours. They'll all be under you.
Market, harbour, assembly-place: all yours.
Councillors? Walk all over them. Generals?
Spit in their eye. Police? Give 'em twenty years.
The town hall's yours, to keep your women in.

AGORAKRITOS.
Me?

DEMOSTHENES.
You. I see you still don't see.
Get up on here.
Now then, what can you see? The sea?

AGORAKRITOS.
Yes.

DEMOSTHENES.
170   The offshore islands?

AGORAKRITOS.
Yes.

DEMOSTHENES.
 The markets? The merchant-ships?

AGORAKRITOS.
 Yes.

DEMOSTHENES.
 All yours. Are you getting the picture now?
 Have a good look at your empire...a really good look.
 One eye over *here*...the other over *here*...

AGORAKRITOS.
 What's the good of an empire, if I go cross-eyed?

DEMOSTHENES.
 Cross-eyed, nothing. You'll be a millionaire.
 It's all in the oracle. You'll be the Boss,
 The Man Himself.

AGORAKRITOS.
 You're joking. The Man Himself?
 How can a sausage-seller be the Man Himself?

DEMOSTHENES.
 Because of your background. You're an expert in
  tripe.   180
 You're vulgar, loudmouthed, low – just what you
  need
 For a career in politics.

AGORAKRITOS.
 But I don't deserve...

DEMOSTHENES.
 Don't *deserve?* What d'you mean, you don't deserve?
 What are you, a gentleman?

AGORAKRITOS.
 Me? No: scum.

DEMOSTHENES.
 Exactly: scum. Just right for public life.

AGORAKRITOS.
Look, mate, I never had no education,
Never went to school. I mean, I can read a *bit*...

DEMOSTHENES.
Keep it dark! It could ruin everything.
We don't want honest men, who can read a bit,
190   To lead the people. We want lowdown scum
And swine. It's all yours. Grab your chance!
The gods have handed it to you on a plate,
Here in the oracle.

AGORAKRITOS.
What oracle? What does it say?

DEMOSTHENES.
Here, look. It's a kind of riddle. Listen.
WHEN THE LEATHERY EAGLE, OLD
    CROOKED-CLAWS,
SWOOPS DOWN ON THE LOWDOWN SNAKE-
    IN-THE-GRASS,
THE BLOOD-SUCKER, YEA VERILY, THEN
    SHALL THE BRINE
AND THE PAPHLAGON'S TANNERY-ACIDS
    BEGONE,
200   AND A HEAVENLY HALO SURROUND MEN
    OF TRIPE –
That is, unless they go on *selling sausages*.

AGORAKRITOS.
I don't get it. What's that to do with me?

DEMOSTHENES.
'The leathery eagle': that's Paphlagon.

AGORAKRITOS.
'Old crooked-claws'?

DEMOSTHENES.
Speaks for itself.
Old crooked-claws goes everywhere, grabs
    everything.

AGORAKRITOS.
  But what's this 'snake-in-the-grass'?

DEMOSTHENES.
  That's obvious.
  Snakes are long and wriggly – so are sausages.
  Snakes are slithery and horrible – so's tripe.
  There's going to be a fight. Eagle and snake.
  And snake wins...IF HE GETS THE POINT IN
      TIME!   210

AGORAKRITOS.
  It's about me, isn't it, that oracle?
  But how can I rule? All I know is tripe.

DEMOSTHENES.
  The recipe's the same. You won't have to change
  A thing. You stir things up, you mangle and mince
  And make a total hash of everything.
  You sugar the customers with honeyed words
  To whet their appetites. You make full use
  Of your natural gifts: you're vulgar and loud
  And low. Everything fits – the oracles,
  The stars, the gods. Come here. Put on your crown.

  He crowns him with a string of sausages.

  And have a drink.   220
  To Thick-as-two-short-planks. Up yours!
  All right: he's all yours.

AGORAKRITOS.
  Just a minute. I'm not doing it all on my own.
  I'll need some help. Who's on my side?
  All the Top People here are yellow...
  And all the Bottom People too.

DEMOSTHENES.
  There are a thousand Knights[13] who hate his guts.
  They'll help. Plus every honest citizen.
  Plus all this educated audience.
  Plus me. And the god as well. We'll lend a hand.

230   In any case, you won't see Kle...er, HIM
In person. The mask-makers were all too scared
To model him. But everyone sitting here
Will recognise him. No one here's a fool.

AGORAKRITOS.
Oh my god! Help! I think he's coming out.

Roaring and crashing from inside. PAPHLAGON
storms out.

PAPHLAGON.
Where are you? Traitors! Spies! You'll pay for this!
By the Twelve Great Gods: Zeus...Hera...Poseidon...
Athene...Apollo...Hermes...Hey! What's this?
A wine-jug? An *enemy* wine-jug? I knew it.
Don't move, wherever you are. We've got you.
The whole place is surrounded. You're done for now.

DEMOSTHENES (*to* AGORAKRITOS).
240   Hey, come back. Where are you going? Our saviour,
Our sausage-seller. Don't go! Don't run away!

PAPHLAGON *advances on them.*

Help! He-e-e-e-elp! Where are you, Knights?
Hurry up! It's now or never. Come and help!

Trumpet calls and cavalry noises off. DEMOSTHENES
tries to put some nerve into AGORAKRITOS.

There you are. They're coming. Stand up to him.
Look him in the eye. Look: dust. They're coming.
Hit him, punch him, kick him, spit in his eye...

Enter CHORUS OF KNIGHTS.

CHORUS.
On! On! On! Hunt him, ride him down,
Bounder, cad, rotter, sneak,
Reptile, hell-hound, vulture, cur,
Ruffian, bully, jailbird, scum,
You hound, you hound, you hound,
(He really is an utter hound).

Give him a wigging, six of the best,   250
A tanning, a beating, a thrashing.
Horsewhip the bounder, that's my advice.
Tally-ho! He's gone away.
A loose fish, an oily rag,
A slippery eel...he's in politics.
Don't lose him. Thrash the bounder now.

PAPHLAGON (*to the audience*).
Ladies and gentlemen, help! I'm on your side;
Remember my election manifesto?
'I'll scream, and scream, and scream
Till I get what the people want.'
A democrat. And now
These traitors are beating me up. Come and help!

CHORUS.
Oh I say, look here. You eat your way
Through public funds, you finger the taxes,
You squeeze the officials to see who's green,   260
Who's ready to fall, who's ripe;
You like them rich and juicy, hiding away
From public life; you pick 'em and skin 'em
And squeeze 'em and spit out the pips –

PAPHLAGON.
Don't hit me, sir. I'm on your side. O master,
What about a statue in the park...for bravery?

CHORUS.
Get up. Don't crawl. What d'you take us for –
Old men? You won't wriggle out that way.   270
Grab him, chaps. Round here, that's right. Look out!
He's makin' a dash for it. Quick! Head him off!

PAPHLAGON.
Democracy! Power to the people! Help!
The pigs! The brutes! They've kicked me in the guts.

CHORUS.
Screaming and yelling. That's all you ever do.

AGORAKRITOS, sure that PAPHLAGON is safely held, swaggers forward.

AGORAKRITOS.
It's all right now. I'm here.

PAPHLAGON.
I'll shout *you* down.

CHORUS.
All right. If you shout him down, you win.
But if he's a filthier swine, *we* win.

PAPHLAGON.
That traitor! That spy! I know his game:
Smuggling black puddings to the enemy.

AGORAKRITOS.
280   And what about you? Sneaking into the dining room
Empty-handed, and then out with a bellyful...

DEMOSTHENES.
That's right: loaves of bread, joints of meat,
    sardines –
Not even Perikles could stuff it away like him.

PAPHLAGON.
Now you've had it. Both of you.

AGORAKRITOS.
I'll shout three times as loud.

PAPHLAGON.
A hundred times as loud.

AGORAKRITOS.
A hundred million times.

PAPHLAGON.
Just try a fight. I'll *tell*.

AGORAKRITOS.
I'll lick you like a dog.

PAPHLAGON.
290   I'll turn you inside out.

AGORAKRITOS.
I'll slice you into bits.

PAPHLAGON.
Just look me in the eye.

AGORAKRITOS.
I'm just as low as you.

PAPHLAGON.
Tell-tale! I'll beat you up.

AGORAKRITOS.
Dung-heap! I'll sweep you up.

PAPHLAGON.
I'm a proper thief, not you.

AGORAKRITOS.
It's me that's a thief, not you.

PAPHLAGON.
I'm a bigger one than you.

AGORAKRITOS.
You said it, mate, not me.

PAPHLAGON.
You...you...! Just wait! You'll see.
I'll tell. These pig-guts here...   300
Have they paid sausage tax?

CHORUS.
Disgusting, loudmouthed scum!
Muck-peddler! Conman! Bum!
You make everyone sick.
You know every low trick.
You bellow and roar and howl;   310
You demand
Cash in hand;
You're vile! You stink! You're foul!

PAPHLAGON.
You've sewn this up already – and I know where.

AGORAKRITOS.
'You've sewn this up...' I've stuffed my sausages!
What do *you* know about sewing? Reject hide,
Cut slanting to look like proper leather shoes.
Size ten in the morning, by evening size twenty-two.

DEMOSTHENES.
That's right. I bought a pair of those. Top quality!
320   Well, it gave the neighbours a laugh. I went for a
    walk,
And halfway home you'd have thought I was doing
    the crawl.

CHORUS (*to* PAPHLAGON, *in two separate groups*).
You're an expert in bare-faced cheek
    The patron saint of politics.
You've used it to milk the city dry
    You've even made Archeptolemos cry.
330   Yes, you aimed high; but he'll aim higher
    Your time is past –
A bigger cheat, a bigger liar
    Thank god, at last!
Now then, we know you're scum –
    Like the best in the nation.
Show us you're not so dumb –
    Who needs an education?

AGORAKRITOS.
All right, I'll tell you what sort of citizen he is.

PAPHLAGON.
Let me speak first.

AGORAKRITOS.
No chance. I'm bigger scum than you.

CHORUS.
You tell him. Your Daddy and Grandad were scum
    as well.

PAPHLAGON.
You'd better let me speak first.

AGORAKRITOS.
No chance.

PAPHLAGON.
You'd better.

AGORAKRITOS.
All right, let's discuss it. I'll speak first.

PAPHLAGON.
I'll *burst*.

AGORAKRITOS.
No chance.   340

CHORUS.
Go on, for god's sake let him burst.

PAPHLAGON.
What makes you think you can argue with me, and win?

AGORAKRITOS.
I can mix arguments, as hot as mustard sauce.

PAPHLAGON.
Mix arguments? You're not serving sausages now,
Catfood and gristle mashed up in slimy sauce.
You know what you are? An amateur, like all the
    rest.
You're asked to give a speech, and you're up all
    night
Walking the streets, practising, muttering to
    yourself,
Waving your arms about, sipping water and
    showing off
To your friends. A speaker – you? You must be   350
    raving mad.

AGORAKRITOS (*gesturing at the audience*).
And what do you swallow, to make them swallow
    you?
They're all struck dumb. You're like the kiss of
    death.

PAPHLAGON.
>Oh no, I'm not. I'm unique. I'm like nothing else.
>>I'm me.
>I can eat a whole fried whale, with a barrel of wine,
>And still have the guts to shout the generals down.

AGORAKRITOS.
>I can eat a ton of tripe, a mile of sausages,
>Washed down with the water I boiled them in,
>And still choke your speakers, before I wash my
>>hands.

CHORUS.
360   Is this a private feast? Can anyone join in?

PAPHLAGON.
>Can *you* eat herring, and mash the allies up?

AGORAKRITOS.
>Can *you* eat beef, and embezzle a silver mine?

PAPHLAGON.
>I'll chew the Assembly up and spit it out.

AGORAKRITOS.
>I'll strip your guts to use as sausage-skins.

PAPHLAGON.
>I'll grab your arse and turn it inside out.

CHORUS.
>If you grab his arse, you'll have to grab mine first.

PAPHLAGON.
>I'll tie you in knots.

AGORAKRITOS.
>I'll tear you to bits.

PAPHLAGON.
>I'll tan your hide.

AGORAKRITOS.
370   I'll stuff your guts.

PAPHLAGON.
  I'll peg you out.

AGORAKRITOS.
  I'll mince you up.

PAPHLAGON.
  I'll pluck your hairs.

AGORAKRITOS.
  I'll pierce your ears.

DEMOSTHENES.
  Grab him and make him open wide;
  Rip out his tongue, look down inside
  At his measly tum   380
  And spotty bum.

CHORUS.
  He's dangerous. He's quick.
  He knows every dirty trick.
  He'll gouge and tear and jab,
  So before he makes a grab
  Get at him. Get in first.
  Tenderise him,
  Pulverise him;
  Fight dirty; do your worst.   390

AGORAKRITOS.
  He's yellow. He hasn't changed since the day he
      was born.
  Remember those Spartan prisoners – hidden away
  Like porridge oats till he was ready to sell them back?
  That's typical. What a hero! What a superman!

PAPHLAGON.
  You don't scare me. Not while the council-chamber
      lives,
  And Demos sits and goggles, like he's always done.

CHORUS (in two separate groups, as before).
  Will nothing get under his skin?
        Will nothing make him blush?

D'you like him?
                    I'd rather go to bed
400   With Kratinos. I'd rather be dead.
Like a bluebottle, buzzing around
                    From flower to flower,
Spewing profits all over the ground
                    In a golden shower.
Quick! Swat him! Squash him flat!
                    Don't let him get away.
I'll drink a toast to that.
410   Isn't this a lovely play?

PAPHLAGON.
    You'll never be a bigger scum than me. No chance.
    What, lose to you? I'd rather give up politics.

AGORAKRITOS.
    You'll lose. I've got the background for it:
        butcher's knives,
    Thick ears, and years and years of eating rich
        men's scraps.

PAPHLAGON.
    Scraps, like a dog? And you think I'll give in to you?
    I'm a bulldog, mate, a gorilla. Look at these teeth.

AGORAKRITOS.
    I know what's what. I learned in the cookhouse,
        every trick.
    I was hardly *so* high, when I learned how to shout,
    'Look! There! The first cuckoo of spring!' They all
        looked up,
    And I pinched a piece of steak, right under their
420   noses.

CHORUS.
    I say, you know, that's damned clever. A piece of
        steak?
    Like chaps who eat oysters when there's no R in
        the month.

AGORAKRITOS.
    They never caught me, neither. If they came looking,
    I hid the steak up my crutch and swore blind it
        wasn't me.
    One of them politicians saw me once, and said,
    'That boy's got a future. He'll lead the state one
        day.'

CHORUS.
    Well, how could he doubt it? You were standing there
    Red-handed, telling lies, with a steak stuffed up
        your crutch.

PAPHLAGON.
    Shut up, both of you! I'll deal with you.   430
    I'm an earthquake, a hurricane, a thunderstorm...

AGORAKRITOS.
    Dirty weather, eh? I'll reef in my sausages,
    And pull for shelter. You blow yourself inside out.

DEMOSTHENES.
    I'll bail him with this, if he starts to spring a leak.

PAPHLAGON (*to him*).
    You old fool! That pile of cash you stole – I'll tell!

DEMOSTHENES.
    Look out, he's blowing a gale of lies. Drop anchor,
        quick!

PAPHLAGON.
    Ten silver pieces: I know you've got them stacked
        away.

DEMOSTHENES.
    What's the matter? Do I give you one to shut your
        mouth?

AGORAKRITOS.
    That's what he wants, the swine. Let go the ropes
        a bit.   440
    The wind's dropping.

PAPHLAGON.
> You're going to be sorry for this.
> You're going to be really sorry.

AGORAKRITOS.
> 'Really sorry'? Dear oh dear,
> What a nasty little boy!

PAPHLAGON.
> Listen to him! Lord Muck!

AGORAKRITOS.
> And who are you? Big Dick?

PAPHLAGON.
> You bastard!

AGORAKRITOS.
450 Swine!

CHORUS.
> Go on. Poke him in the eye.

PAPHLAGON (*to the audience*).
> I've had it.
> They're *all* in this.

CHORUS.
> Rah! Rah! Rah! Rah!
> Fight! Fight! Fight! Fight!
> Crown him with *this*.
> Smother him with *this*.

> *Battle royal. At last* PAPHLAGON *yields, and the*
> CHORUS *congratulate* AGORAKRITOS.

CHORUS.
> Brave guts! Proud paunch! O belly supreme,
> Our saviour, the dawn of our brave new world,
> Look: he's completely floored by your arguments.
460 How shall I praise you? How express my joy?

PAPHLAGON.
> By god, d'you think I didn't *know* this plan
> Was being put together on the drawing-board?

CHORUS (*to the audience*).
Hear that? Thinks he's some kind of architect.

AGORAKRITOS.
What made you think you'd get away with it?
A secret pact, hammered out with the enemy –

CHORUS (*to the audience*).
This one's a blacksmith. Where will it end?   470

AGORAKRITOS.
All you want is a good price for those prisoners,
Those porridge oats. Well, you haven't a chance.
I'm going to the Assembly, to tell the people now –
And no money in all the world will stop my
    mouth.

PAPHLAGON.
You wait! I'll get to the Assembly first,
And spill the beans about *you*: black-market deals
With Foreign Powers in the middle of the night...
Cheese-paring and haggling with Theban thugs –

AGORAKRITOS.
What *is* the latest price for Theban cheese?   480

PAPHLAGON.
I'll cheese you! I'll flatten you! You wait!

Exit.

CHORUS.
Well, don't just stand there. Think of something, quick.
Remember where you said you stuffed that steak?
Get down to the Assembly fast, before
He starts yelling and hurling lies about.

AGORAKRITOS.
All right, all right. I've got to get my tripe
And my chopping-knives tidy, haven't I?

DEMOSTHENES.
Grease yourself with this. Go on, rub it in.   490
Then you can slide away if things get tough.

CHORUS (*to the audience*).
Now *this* one thinks he's an athletics coach.

DEMOSTHENES.
Now swallow this.

AGORAKRITOS.
What is it?

DEMOSTHENES.
Mustard. You want to get steamed up, don't you?
Come on, come on.

AGORAKRITOS.
I'm coming.

DEMOSTHENES (*as they go*).
Remember:
Fight dirty. Hit below the belt. Bite. Gouge.
Grap hold of his wattles, and rip them off...

Exeunt.

CHORUS.
Goodbye! Good luck!
We're all behind you,
500 And Hermes, god of cheats...
Go down, and win
A victor's crown.

(*to the audience*)

Ladies and gentlemen, your attention please.
It's Chorus Time. You've been waiting for this.
I mean, you're such an educated lot...

Short dance. Then:

CHORUS[14].
If a comedy playwright of old
Had invited us here to take part
In his play, to appear on the stage,
We'd have turned him down flat. But this man,
510 Aristophanes, shares our dislikes,
Tells the truth, and courageously rides

In the teeth of the whirlwind and storm.
Aristophanes: yes, that's the name.
Are you puzzled? Not heard it before?
Why's he kept it so dark? Is he shy
Or just lazy? I'll try to explain.
He's in show business. Comedy's tough,
Doesn't fall for the first man who asks.
And the audience is tougher. He knows
That your praise is like blossom in spring:
Very nice while it lasts. But when spring
Turns to autumn, you don't want to know:
When your heroes are past it, they're dead.
Look at Magnes: the best in the bunch,   520
Till the grey hairs of autumn appeared.
D'you remember his choruses? *Lydians, Birds,*
Harpists, Frogs...he had hundreds of hits.
Tell me, where is he now? Or just think
Of Kratinos, a torrent of jokes
Bubbling over and sweeping away
All his rivals, like twigs in a storm.
Every party you went to, they sang
'Doro, sandalled in figs...', 'The Music-Men...' –   530
Who remembers them now that he's old,
Now the joints of his genius are cracked
And the strings out of tune? You don't care
That he's senile and sodden with drink,
Not respected and given a seat
In the theatre, there beside the god.
Need I mention the treatment you gave
Poor old Krates? The hisses? The boos?
Hardly banquets, his plays: more like snacks
Of the driest, most delicate wit.
But they lasted – or lasted till now.   540
Makes you shudder? Our author was right
To hang back. Practise handling the boat,
Learn the ropes, keep an eye on the wind:
Then you're ready to sail. Was he right
Not to jump up and shoot off his mouth?

(in one breath)

Is he leading the race? Give a cheer
As he rounds the last bend
And comes thundering home.
Let him win the first prize;
Send him home with a glow
Like a bonfire, a gleam
550 On his lofty, bald head.

Poseidon, lord of horses, come!
You delight in hooves clattering,
Horses whinnying, swift hulls
Hissing through dark water,
The gleam of chariots
Flashing, crashing past;
Lord of Sounion, dolphin-king,
560 Son of Kronos, god of gods,
Protector of Athens, come down
And smile on our play today.

Short dance. Then:

Praise to our fathers, the Knights of old:
Brave men to a man, fine patriots,
Victors everywhere on land and sea,
An ornament, a credit to the state.
They didn't stop to count the enemy:
570 It was 'Up and at 'em! Tally ho!'
If you fell on your face, up you jumped,
Dusted yourself off, and galloped on
As if nothing had happened. Stout chaps!
They didn't care tuppence for rewards
And medals – not like today: unless
Your pay's guaranteed, you just won't fight.
That's not our way. We fight for the gods
And the honour of Athens, not cash.
We ask just one reward: when we've won,
580 Don't grudge us hot baths and curly hair.

Queen of this holy city, come!
Athene our protector, you rule
A lovely land, a people proud
In war, supreme in the arts;
Bring us victory, on land
And sea – and here today.
Don't let our enemies win!   590
Support us, breathe over us
Your skill, your power to win.
Athene, come down to us today.

Praise to our horses, our gallant steeds.
What fine mounts! What splendid patriots!
They carried us all without complaint
On route-marches, and in battle too;
And when the word came through to embark,
They pranced on board with their metal cups
And army rations. They sat right down   600
On the rowing benches with the men,
Took hold of the oars, and whinnied, 'Hup!
On, Dapple, on! Gee up! Haul away!'
At Corinth, off they cantered. The young
Colts, the yearlings, fetched the fodder in –
Crabs, it was, instead of foreign oats:
Little crabs, hoofed up pincers and all.
In the end, the enemy, caught up
In a pincer-movement, showed the white flag.   610

Dance. When it ends, enter AGORAKRITOS.

CHORUS.
My dear chap! Stout fella! What a brick!
We've been in such a stew...on tenterhooks...
What happened? Did you win?
Did you knock 'em for six?

AGORAKRITOS.
For six? I knocked 'em for *ninety*-six.

CHORUS.
Magnificent! Super! Oh, jolly good!

What a hero! You keep your promises.
Tell us what happened,
There's a good chap.
620   Take us through it, step by step.
Don't be modest. We're dying to hear.

AGORAKRITOS.
It's worth hearing, too. The whole story.
I got to the Assembly, right on his heels,
And he was at it already: spewing out
Thunder and lightning, volcanoes of words –
A load of rubbish about you Knights,
Like you was spies and traitors to the state.
The councillors were sitting there like sausages
630   Being stuffed, all mustard looks and flapping ears.
You could see he had them where he wanted them.
They believed every word. I thought to myself,
'By all the powers that be, by liars and cheats
And pickpockets and frauds and filthy swine,
By the market-place that made me what I am,
Is he going to get away with it? No!
Not while I've a tongue, and a throat, and a cheek.'
I was thinking that, when some bastard
Farted on the right. 'Right,' I thought, 'the wind's
640   Behind you. On you go.' So I pushed my behind
Through the railings and really opened up.
'Latest!' I shouted. 'Latest! Hear all about it!
Good news for the council. Sardines going cheap.
Merchants blame war-conditions. Prices slashed.'
You should have seen their faces. Sardines, cheap!
They wanted to give me a vote of thanks.
I gave them a tip, from the horse's mouth:
'You want to corner all the sardines in town?
650   Go down to Potter's Row, and buy up every jar.'
They gaped at me, and clapped their hands.
Mind you, that Paphlagon's no fool. He knew my
      game –
And he knew what the Assembly wanted, too.
'Gentlemen,' he said, 'what we ought to do

To celebrate this news, is sacrifice
A hundred oxen to Athene, and have
A great big party.' Bullshit, that's what it was:
Anyone could see that. So I jumped up, and said,   660
'Two hundred oxen, and a thousand goats
To Artemis tomorrow, providing – *providing* –
Pilchards are still a penny a hundredweight.'
That brought them round to me again – and he
Started fuming and stamping and gibbering
Till they had to call the cops to calm him down.
All the councillors were yelling for pilchards,
And he kept bawling, 'Wait a minute! No!
What about the conference, the peace-debate?
The Spartan delegation's just outside.'
'Peace-conference?' they shouted back. 'They don't   670
Want peace, they want to get their thieving hands
On our sardines. No peace! Let the war go on!'
And they voted to jack the Assembly in,
And started jumping over the railing...so I
Ran down to the market-place, and bought
Every stalk of coriander, every leek
In sight. (*Coriander*...goes well with *fish*.)
I started handing it out to the councillors...
For free. That did the trick. They yelled and
     cheered,   680
And now I'm Public Hero Number One,
Thanks to some coriander and a bunch of leeks.

CHORUS.
Magnificent! Super! You're bound to go far.
He's a slippery dog, a blackguard, a crook,
But it's curtains for him now.
You'll put him in the shade.
Bring out your master-plan:
We're right behind you. Fight, and win.   690

AGORAKRITOS.
Paphlagon's coming – look! Like a tidal wave,
Boiling and bubbling and foaming at the mouth.
He's after me. Big bully! See if I care.

Enter PAPHLAGON.

PAPHLAGON.
Right. Now you're for it. I'll tell on you.
I'll get you. I'll smash you in, or burst.

AGORAKRITOS.
You, smash *me* in? Don't make me laugh.
Windbag! Compost-heap!

He blows a raspberry.

PAPHLAGON.
I'll swallow you whole and spit you out.

AGORAKRITOS.
700   I'll drink you at a gulp, and belch you up.

PAPHLAGON.
I've booked a front seat for your funeral.

AGORAKRITOS.
This is the only seat you'll get.

PAPHLAGON.
I'll put you inside. I'll sell you like a slave.

AGORAKRITOS.
Look who's talking. What is it? Like some of *this*?

PAPHLAGON.
I'll rip out your guts. I'll tear you apart.

AGORAKRITOS.
Oh, go and cut your nails. And shut your face.

PAPHLAGON.
710   I'm going to tell Demos. You'll pay for this.

AGORAKRITOS.
You've got him in your pocket, haven't you?

PAPHLAGON.
Don't you worry. I know what the People wants.

AGORAKRITOS.
You're just like a bloody nursemaid, aren't you?

You chew up the People's food, nice and soft –
And gulp three-quarters of it down yourself.

PAPHLAGON.
He's putty in my hands. I manage him.
I work him: open and shut, open and shut...   720

AGORAKRITOS.
Yes, I do the same – with my behind.

PAPHLAGON.
Because of that Assembly, you think you've won.
But the People's mine.

AGORAKRITOS.
All right, let's go and see.
Come on, then! What are you waiting for?

PAPHLAGON (*knocking on* DEMOS' *door*).
De-mos... De-mos... Please come out.

AGORAKRITOS (*knocking*).
De-mos... master,
Father... Please come out...

PAPHLAGON.
O Demos, O *sir*,
They're being horrid to me. Please come out.

The door opens, and DEMOS *comes out.*

DEMOS.
Who's making all this noise? Go away.
You're messing up the flowers.
Oh. Paphlagon.
What is it? What's wrong?

PAPHLAGON.
They're beating me up,   730
Him, and those Knights...because of you.

DEMOS.
Me? Why?

PAPHLAGON.
I'm loyal and devoted. I *love* you, sir.

DEMOS (*to* AGORAKRITOS).
Who are *you*, then?

AGORAKRITOS.
His rival. I love you too.
Oh sir, I've so wanted to do my bit
To help – like every other honest man.
But we can't get near you. *He's* always in the way.
You behave like one of them fancy-boys:
You never go out with honest, decent men,
740   Just scum – cobblers, lamp-pedlars, *tanners*...

PAPHLAGON.
I've served the People, haven't I?

AGORAKRITOS.
Yeah? How?

PAPHLAGON.
I cut in on those generals after Pylos,
And brought those Spartan prisoners home in
    chains.

AGORAKRITOS.
I cut in on the cooks from the kitchen,
And grabbed a plate of someone else's stew.

PAPHLAGON.
Look, sir, why not settle it, here and now?
Sit here and judge which one of us loves you best.

AGORAKRITOS.
Oh no you don't. Not here! Anywhere but here!

DEMOS.
750   Of course, here. I *like* it here. This here
Is *my* place, where the People always meets[15].

AGORAKRITOS (*to the audience*).
That's done it. He's quite bright inside, at home,
On his own. But once he has to bend his mind

To politics, out here, his brains go soft
And his mouth gapes open, as if he was sucking figs.

Bustle of preparation. A chair is set for
DEMOS, *and* AGORAKRITOS *and* PAPHLAGON
take their places on either side of him.

CHORUS.
Quick! Batten the hatches, slacken sail,
Break out your arguments, your net
Of words. He's sharp and mean and sly.
Thunder and lightning! Swamp! Destroy!   760

(*to* AGORAKRITOS)

Get your grappling-irons ready, to board
Him and cripple his ship. Get in first!

PAPHLAGON (*praying*).
Queen Athene, if I win this fight,
If I prove I love Demos the best,
Let me go on doing nothing (like now);
Let me scrounge off the people (like now).
For if he loves him best, and I lose,
I'll be sliced up and made into shoes.

AGORAKRITOS (*praying*).
Master Demos, if *he* wins this fight,
If he loves you the best, chop me up   770
Into mincemeat and grate me like cheese,
Slice my bollocks and serve them for tea.

PAPHLAGON.
Master Demos, there's no one on Earth
As devoted as me. When I came,
I took charge of your money. I squeezed
And tormented and begged – just for you.

AGORAKRITOS.
What's so great about that? I could steal,
I could butter another man's bread.
It's not you that he loves, it's himself
And his seat by the fire. Look at you: 780

The great hero of Marathon, sat
On a stone. Does he care? Does he hell!
But *I've* brought you a cushion. Lift up
That distinguished behind. There you are.

DEMOS.
My dear boy! Did you tell me your name?
What a patriot! Loyal and true...

PAPHLAGON (*aside to* AGORAKRITOS).
You soon found the right way to his heart.

AGORAKRITOS (*aside to him*).
790   It's a well-trodden path. *You* should know.

PAPHLAGON (*to* DEMOS).
Sir, there's no one who loves you like me.
I'm devoted. I'm loyal. Your best friend.

AGORAKRITOS.
His best friend? You refused to make peace.
Eight long years you refused, while *his* friends,
Refugees from the country, were forced
To make homes out of barrels and crates.
When ambassadors came to make peace
All you gave them was kicks on the bum.

PAPHLAGON.
I was thinking of *him*. Look: this war
Must go on till he conquers all Greece.
He's the champ, and I'm keeping him fit.
800   I'm his trainer. I see that he wins.

AGORAKRITOS.
You don't want him to win. You want bribes
And extortion and plunder for *you*.
Keep the war going: it's making you rich.
Keep the People half-starved, in the dark,
Worried stiff, in the palm of your hand.
Once there's peace, he'll go back to his farm,
Build his strength up on porridge and greens –
And discover just how he's been had.

Then you'll suffer: he'll call out the dogs
And come looking for trouble. So cheat
While you can. Stuff him silly with dreams.

PAPHLAGON.

Sir, don't listen. It's slander and lies.   810
I'm your saviour, your hero, your friend.
I'm a second Themistokles, me.

AGORAKRITOS.

Did you hear him? Themistokles, now!
He put jam on our bread, saved our bacon,
Put cream in our milk – not like you
With your programme of soft soap and crumbs.
And he went into exile. Will you?

PAPHLAGON.

Master Demos, don't listen. You *know*   820
How I love you –

DEMOS.

Don't touch me! You swine!
All these years, and I never...you *swine!*

AGORAKRITOS.

Dear old Demos, you've got it at last!
He's a conman, a crook.
While you're snoozing, he grabs
All the titbits himself,
While he ladles the cash
From your private account.

PAPHLAGON.

You shut up, or I'll tell
How you fingered the till –

AGORAKRITOS.

Oh, stop dancing about.   830
They all know you're a crook.
Shall I show them the place
Where you hide all your cash,

> All those enemy bribes
> For betraying the state?

CHORUS.

> What a clever reply! What a man!
> Our saviour, greatest of Greeks!
> The Man Himself, the lord of all,
> The captain of the ship of state.

840

> (*to* AGORAKRITOS)

> Don't give up now. He's given you an opening.
> Use your muscles. Get a stranglehold. You're
> bound to win.

PAPHLAGON.

> Oh no he's not. By Poseidon! I'll deal with him.
> I've still got my greatest triumph up my sleeve,
> The one that makes all my enemies stand and gape.
> Yes, Pylos. Till the shields rot, we'll remember
> that.[16]

AGORAKRITOS.

> Hang on, hang on. Those shields give me a
> stranglehold.
> If you loved the People as much as you say you did,
> Why did you hang them up with the handles on?
> You get it, sir? It's a plot. To stop you getting him,
> He's got a whole gang of toughs: cheese-graters,
> grocers,
> Honey-blenders, cobblers, all trained for just one
> thing:
> The minute you get that banishing-look, they move
> in,
> Grab hold of those shields, and fence off the
> market-place.

850

DEMOS.

> Oh no! I didn't notice they still had handles on.
> You swine! You've robbed and double-crossed us
> long enough.

PAPHLAGON.

> Dear, kind master, you don't want to listen to *him*.   860
> Can't you see I'm the best friend you'll ever have?
> Who is it that sniffs out all them terrorists, them
> *Coups d'état?* Who is it that yells and saves your guts?

AGORAKRITOS.

> Terrorists! *Coups d'état!* You're like them fishermen
> Who go looking for eels. If they find nothing there,
> If the waters are calm, they ferret about in mud
> And slime till they find what they want – like you
> And your bribes. Just look at you, the biggest cobbler
> For miles around – and you won't even spare a patch
> For his old sandals.

DEMOS.

> Hey, that's right. He never has.   870

AGORAKRITOS.

> Well, what d'you expect, from *him*? Look: *I've* brought
> you these.
> Just try them on. That's right. How are they? Do
> they fit?[17]

DEMOS (*to the* CHORUS).

> Now *he's* what I call generous, a real patriot.
> He knows what the People want...*and* their poor
> old feet.

PAPHLAGON.

> A pair of shoes, and you forget all I've done for you!
> Who pasted the poofs, eh? Who settled Gryttos' hash?

AGORAKRITOS.

> Poofs? Been looking for poofs, have you? What for?
> Afraid they might go into politics? Poofs!   880
> You're so busy with poofs, you didn't notice *him:*
> The People, sitting shivering without a cloak.
> Poor old man...in winter, too. Look: *this* is what he
> needs.

DEMOS.

A cloak. Not even Themistokles thought of that.
He had some good ideas, mind: those wooden
walls, for one.
But if I had to choose, I'd still prefer a cloak.

PAPHLAGON.

You lowdown, cheating swine. Where did you
learn all this?

AGORAKRITOS.

When a man's going out for a drink in a hurry,
He doesn't care *whose* shoes he takes. I'm wearing
yours.

PAPHLAGON.

You'll never win. Out of my way. I'll wrap him in
890   *this*.

DEMOS.

Groo! Get off! Take it away! It stinks!

AGORAKRITOS.

He did that on purpose. He's trying to stink you
out.
And he's done it before. Remember that garlic?

DEMOS.

Will I ever forget it?

AGORAKRITOS.

He bought up all the garlic in town
And gave it out free to every juryman.
Belching and farting... Justice went right up the
spout.

DEMOS.

I remember that. That bog-attendant told me...

AGORAKRITOS.

900   That's right. It was shit-eater's benefit, that day.

DEMOS.

That's him all over, trying to drop us in it –

PAPHLAGON (*to* AGORAKRITOS).
  Bastard!
  Who gave you the idea of using filth like this?

AGORAKRITOS.
  I've told you: *you* did. Your methods. They always win.

PAPHLAGON.
  But not this time. I'll show you. Sir, master, sit back,
  Don't stir. Are you comfy? I'll fetch you a nice plate
    of...cash.

AGORAKRITOS.
  What you need is this little pot, this little jar
  Of ointment. Rub it in, sir. It's for your aching corns.

PAPHLAGON.
  A grey hair! I'll pull it out, and make you young
    again.

AGORAKRITOS.
  This rabbit's foot's for you, sir. So kind to the skin...

PAPHLAGON.
  There, master: blow your nose, and wipe it in my hair. 910

AGORAKRITOS.
  No, mine.

PAPHLAGON.
  No, mine.

  (*to* AGORAKRITOS)

  I'll see to you.
  You can have a warship
  To pay for, all your own,
  Some rotten, stinking hulk
  You'll have to have rebuilt
  From the bilges up.
  That'll sort you out.

CHORUS.
  He's coming to the boil. Look out!   920
  Get a ladle, quick, and bail.

PAPHLAGON.
> I'll squeeze you to death
> With ship-tax and surtax
> And supertax. I'll show you.
> I'll dump you in the soup.

AGORAKRITOS.
> *I'm* not making threats.
> I've a prayer instead.
> A dish of cuttlefish,
> Lovely, sizzling hot.

930
> You're just sitting down,
> Smacking your lips,
> When they call you to speak
> In the Assembly –
> For an enormous great bribe.
> You think you've got time
> To finish the dish and go.
> But a man rushes in
> And tells you you've got to go
> At once, and you gulp it down

940
> To get the cash – and choke.

CHORUS.
> Yay! Jolly good! I like that! Yes! Amen.

DEMOS (*to the audience*).
> He's pretty good. Don't you agree? A real friend
> Of the common people.
> And I do mean common.
> Paphlagon, come here. You said you loved me,
> And I swallowed it. Garlic, onions,
> Pickles, radish, leeks... What were you trying to do,
> Get the wind up? Well, you're sacked. Give me back
> The Great Seal of Office...the pantry key.

PAPHLAGON *hands over a key fixed to a decorated wooden slat.*

PAPHLAGON.

Here. But remember: if you get rid of me   950
You're bound to get someone even worse.

DEMOS.

Hey! This isn't my Great Seal. Is it?
Mine's got my picture on. Not this at all.

AGORAKRITOS.

Let's have a look. What *is* your picture, then?

DEMOS.

Stuffed vine-leaves on a plate. Done to a turn.

AGORAKRITOS.

No vine-leaves.

DEMOS.

No vine-leaves? What *is* there, then?

AGORAKRITOS.

A sort of cormorant, making a speech on a rock.

DEMOS.

Oh my god!

AGORAKRITOS.

What is it?

DEMOS.

Take it away from me!
Not that! Anything but that! Kleonymos!
Here, take this one. From now on, you're the boss.

PAPHLAGON.

Oh sir! No! You can't! Oh please. Not yet.   960

He has a sudden brainwave.

Oracles! Horoscopes! Let me tell your fortune first.

AGORAKRITOS.

I've got horoscopes too.

PAPHLAGON.
Oh yeah? *Mine* say
If you listen to him, you're a pricked balloon.

AGORAKRITOS.
If you listen to him, you're a loony prick.

PAPHLAGON.
My star-chart promises you'll rule the world,
With a crown of roses.

AGORAKRITOS.
My star-chart says
You can have a crown and a purple dress and a
    coach
Made of gold – and go chasing that pansy
    Smikython.

PAPHLAGON.
Go and get it, then. Your star-chart. Go on:
970   Bring it here, and show him where it says all that.

DEMOS.
Ooh, goody. Yes. And you bring yours as well.

PAPHLAGON.
What? Oh. All right.

AGORAKRITOS.
All right. No problem. I agree.

Exeunt.

CHORUS.
What a lovely day. What a day
To remember, for all of us:
The day when Kleon got the chop.
Mind you, he has got a friend or two:
Toothless dodderers, pensioned off
980   To dribble and drool in the market-place.
'We need him. Such a *worthy* man.
Eyes here, eyes there, fingers here,
Fingers there...such a *worthy* man.

He paid the piper and called the tune.   990
He *was* the piper. Marches, marches,
Nothing but marches. War made him rich.

Re-enter PAPHLAGON *and* AGORAKRITOS.

PAPHLAGON.
  Here we are. Star-charts. There are more inside.

AGORAKRITOS.
  I found these in the bog. There are more inside.

DEMOS (*to* PAPHLAGON).
  What are they?

PAPHLAGON.
  Your horoscopes.

DEMOS.
  What, all of them?

PAPHLAGON.
  There are boxfuls more inside.   1000

AGORAKRITOS.
  I've attics and cellars crammed full of these.

DEMOS.
  Which prophets are they? What are their names?

PAPHLAGON.
  These were compiled by the great Bakis himself.

DEMOS.
  What about yours?

AGORAKRITOS.
  His big brother. Fakis.

DEMOS.
  What do yours cover? How far do they go?

PAPHLAGON.
  They cover everything. Athens...Pylos...
  You...me...everything.   1010

DEMOS.
What about yours?

AGORAKRITOS.
Oh, it's all in here. Athens...porridge oats...
Sparta...why grocers cheat...the price of fish...
You...me...everything. The whole world's in here.

DEMOS (*to* PAPHLAGON).
Read yours first. I specially like that bit
Where it calls me an eagle, soaring on high.

PAPHLAGON.
All right. Pin your ears back and listen to this.
SON OF ERECHTHEUS, PONDER THE
SOLEMN WORDS
OF APOLLO, THUNDERED FROM THE
TRIPOD IN THE SHRINE.
KEEP SAFE (HE SAID) THE WATCHDOG OF
THE STATE,
WHO SNARLETH AND BARKETH AND
SPLITTETH HIS GUTS
FOR THE SAKE OF YOUR CASH. OH, BEWARE
LEST HE GO,
1020   FOR THE RAVEN (THAT HATETH YOU BOTH)
CROAKETH NOW.

DEMOS.
I don't get it. Erechtheus...watchdog
Of the state...raven...What does it mean?

PAPHLAGON.
I'm the watchdog, aren't I? I bark for you.
Apollo says to look after the watchdog: me.

AGORAKRITOS (*grabbing the roll*).
That's not what it says at all. You want to watch
Your watchdog. He's got his teeth into *this*
For a start. Look.
No, *this* is the one. Mine. *This* one
Puts you straight about watchdogs right away.

DEMOS.

Well, read it, then. Just wait till I get a stone,
In case *his* watchdog-oracle starts to bite.

AGORAKRITOS.

SON OF ERECHTHEUS, LOOK OUT FOR
   KERBEROS   1030
THE SNATCHER, WHO WAGGETH HIS TAIL
   AS YOU EAT,
BUT AS SOON AS YOUR HEAD'S TURNED,
   GOBBLETH YOUR MEAT,
AND AT NIGHT SLIPPETH INTO THE PANTRY,
   AND LICKS –
ER, LICKETH – CLEAN ALL THE ISLANDS IN
   SIGHT.

DEMOS.

Fakis said that? He's much better. He's really good.

PAPHLAGON.

No, sir, no. Listen to this one, and then decide.
FOR LO! TO A WOMAN OF ATHENS A LION
   WILL BE BORN,
THE FLY-WHISK, THE MOSQUITO-SWATTER
   OF THE STATE.
BUILD WOOD ON WOOD, PILE IRON ON
   IRON,
TO KEEP HIM SAFE.   1040
There. Did you follow that?

DEMOS.

Eh? No.

PAPHLAGON.

He says you've got to look after me. I'm Lion.

DEMOS.

You're lyin', eh? I believe that. That's the truth.

AGORAKRITOS.

There's a bit he hasn't read you. Here, look,

Where it talks about these piles of iron
And wood, and what they're supposed to make.

DEMOS.
What does it say?

AGORAKRITOS.
It says, to keep him safe
You should build a cage and pile him in the zoo.

DEMOS.
1050 Now *that's* one prophecy that might come true.

PAPHLAGON.
Don't listen to him. The raven. He's raving mad.
LOOK AFTER THE HAWK, THE LOYAL HAWK
WHO HOOKED HIS TALONS IN THE SPARTAN
  CROWS.

AGORAKRITOS.
Look after Paphlagon, you mean, the bold, brave
  drunk.
O.K., Bigmouth, so you picked up a few Spartans.
What's so brave about that? Even a midget
Looks like a giant, if he rides on a giant's back.

PAPHLAGON.
What *are* you talking about? The oracle refers
To piles. I.e., Pylos. PYLOS ON PYLOS PILED...

DEMOS.
What's he on about now?

AGORAKRITOS.
Piles.

DEMOS.
1060 If he's got piles, he's not going to fill *my* bath.

AGORAKRITOS.
No, no. Piles of loot. He cleans you out, you know.
Look, this is the oracle you really want to hear.
It's about the fleet.

DEMOS.
Go on, I'm listening.
Does it say, for a start, how we *pay* the fleet?

AGORAKRITOS.
BEWARE THE FOXY DOG, MY SON, THE
SHIFTY EYE,
THE PADDING FOOT, THE GREEDY, RUNNY
NOSE.
You know who it means?

DEMOS (*pointing into the audience*).
Yes. Him over there.

AGORAKRITOS.
No, no. Paphlagon. He wants a good fast fleet   1070
To bring the tribute in. The oracle says no.

DEMOS.
I don't get it. What have ships to do with dogs?

AGORAKRITOS.
They're both fast, aren't they?

DEMOS.
Where does the fox come in?

AGORAKRITOS.
Back door of the chicken-house, while you're asleep.

DEMOS.
You still haven't said where I find their pay.

AGORAKRITOS.
I'll find their pay. Give me a day...or three.
Now, here's something else. BEWARE THE
CROOKED CLAW.   1080

DEMOS.
What crooked claw? Is it that hawk again?

AGORAKRITOS.
No: *his* crooked claw. His ever-grabbing hand.

PAPHLAGON.
    Just a minute, just a minute. You'll like this one.
    This is our favourite. LIKE AN EAGLE, SOARING
      HIGH,
    LORD OF THE WHOLE OF GREECE...

AGORAKRITOS.
    Whole of Greece, nothing.
    Mine throws in the Middle East...the whole Red Sea...
    A mountain of Turkish Delight...and all for you.

PAPHLAGON.
1090   I had a dream last night, a prophetic dream.
    Athene came down with a ladle, and poured
    A stream of blessings on Demos' head.

AGORAKRITOS.
    I had a dream last night. Athene came down
    (I could tell it was her because of the owl)
    With a golden flask of pure delight for *you*,
    And a bucket of vinegar to throw over *him*.

DEMOS.
    Stop! Stop!
    Fakis wins. Fakis talks sense. I'm all yours:
    Take me in hand, guide my steps, make me young
      again.

PAPHLAGON.
1100   No, please! Not yet. I'll make some sandwiches.

DEMOS.
    Who wants sandwiches? No thanks.

PAPHLAGON.
    Best white bread...?

AGORAKRITOS.
    I'll make you a trayful of sausage-rolls, black
      puddings,
    Anything you fancy. All you'll have to do is eat.

DEMOS.
  All right, that's the next test. Each of you go in
  And start cooking. The one with the best food wins.

PAPHLAGON (*to* AGORAKRITOS).
  Get out of the way. Me first.

AGORAKRITOS.
  Me first, you mean.   1110

  Exeunt.

CHORUS.
  Look here, Demos, you're a powerful chap.
  I mean, everyone treats you like some sort of king.
  So why d'you let yourself be taken in,
  Flattered, coaxed, persuaded, fooled?
  You swallow every word they say.
  Where's your brain? Here or on holiday?   1120

DEMOS.
  Have you no brain, under all that hair?
  I know what's what. I'm not so dim.
  I *enjoy* being pampered and fed.
  I choose my victim and fatten him up
  On power and theft, till he's good and fat –
  Then I squash him flat, like *that*.   1130

CHORUS.
  So that's how it's done! So that's
  What you're like! You keep a sort
  Of politician-farm here on the Pnyx.
  You fatten them and feed them up
  Till the table's bare, then *crunch!*
  Munch! You gobble them for lunch.   1140

DEMOS.
  Just watch me. I've got my eye on them.
  They think I'm a sucker. They think
  They're really something. But I see all
  Their little thefts. I'm going to ram

A voting paper down their throats one day.
1150   I'll show them. Demos rules, O.K.?

Re-enter PAPHLAGON *and* AGORAKRITOS. *Each carries a basket, filled with plates.*

PAPHLAGON.
    Get knotted, you! Out of the way!

AGORAKRITOS (*pushing ahead, sarcastically*).
    No. After you.

PAPHLAGON.
    Me first, Master Demos. I've been ready
    And eager to serve you for *ages* now.

AGORAKRITOS.
    I've been ready for a hundred years.

PAPHLAGON.
    A thousand years.

DEMOS.
    I've been waiting for a thousand million years.
    I'm sick of both of you.

AGORAKRITOS.
    Ah! You know what we ought to do?

DEMOS.
    Yes. But I'm sure you'll tell me just the same.

AGORAKRITOS.
    We'll start equal.
    A proper race. Me here, him there. You start us off.

DEMOS.
1160   If you must, you must. Get on with it.

    AGORAKRITOS *and* PAPHLAGON *go with their baskets to opposite sides of the stage.*

    Ready?

AGORAKRITOS AND PAPHLAGON.
    Ready.

DEMOS.
  On your marks...set...GO!

AGORAKRITOS.
  This is in the bag.

DEMOS.
  Isn't this *fun?* One blushing bride...two grooms...   1170

PAPHLAGON (*rushing up*).
  You see? I'm first. Here's your favourite chair.

AGORAKRITOS (*darting in ahead of him*).
  Hard luck. I'm firster. Here's your table, sir.

  They settle DEMOS *on the chair at the table, and
  go back to their baskets, for food.*

PAPHLAGON.
  Here's a lovely plate of oat-cakes, baked
  From the porridge oats I picked up at Pylos.

AGORAKRITOS.
  Here's a lovely crusty loaf, baked special,
  Shaped to please Pallas Athene herself.

DEMOS (*turning over the suggestively-shaped loaf*).
  Aye, well. We all know what *she* fancies, now.   1180

PAPHLAGON.
  A bowl of pea-soup, master, piping hot.
  Stirred by the gods. Untouched by human hand.

AGORAKRITOS.
  Stirred by the gods, he says. A plate of soup.

DEMOS.
  Don't mock. The gods, you know: the soup-er powers.

PAPHLAGON.
  A dish of fish.[18]

AGORAKRITOS.
  Some nice, ripe tripe.

DEMOS.
Ugh, tripe!

PAPHLAGON.
1190 A piece of cake.

AGORAKRITOS.
A whole cake, not just a piece.

PAPHLAGON.
A rabbit stew. His favourite.

AGORAKRITOS.
Not rabbit stew!
I can't beat that. Oh god, I've had it now.

PAPHLAGON.
Give in?

AGORAKRITOS.
Of course not. Hey, look! Look over there.
Ambassadors coming, with pots and pots of gold.

PAPHLAGON.
Where? Where?

While his back is turned, **AGORAKRITOS** *grabs the stew.*

AGORAKRITOS.
Oh. Can't you see them?

(*to* DEMOS)

Master...rabbit stew.

PAPHLAGON (*aside to him*).
1200 You can't do that. I made that stew, not you.

AGORAKRITOS (*aside to him*).
Remember Demosthenes...? The Pylos hash?

DEMOS.
My, this is good. Tell me, who cooked it up?

AGORAKRITOS.
It was the gods' idea. But I did the work.

PAPHLAGON.
  I did the cooking. I took all the risks.

DEMOS.   -
  But *he* served it. He gets the thanks. You get...stuffed.

PAPHLAGON.
  I've nothing left! The swine's out-twisted me.

AGORAKRITOS.
  Come on, Demos. It's time to decide.
  Which one of us is best for you and your guts?

DEMOS.
  It isn't easy, in front of all these people.
  I've got to make them see I've chosen right.   1210

AGORAKRITOS.
  That's simple. Come on over here. Shh! Tiptoe.
  Now creep up on my basket, and have a look
  Inside. Then do the same for Paphlagon's.

  DEMOS *turns* AGORAKRITOS' *basket over and
  over, baffled.*

DEMOS.
  I don't get it. What's the point?

AGORAKRITOS.
  It's *empty*, Grandad.
  That's the point. I gave you all I had.

DEMOS.
  I *like* that! A basket on the people's side.

AGORAKRITOS.
  Now try his. Go on.

  DEMOS *picks up* PAPHLAGON's *basket.*

DEMOS.
  Good god, it's still crammed full.
  Look at this monster cake he kept for himself.
  All he gave me was that tiny little bun.   1220

AGORAKRITOS.

> He's been doing that ever since he came to power.
> You get the scraps, and he keeps the best himself.

DEMOS (*to* PAPHLAGON).

> Ungrateful swine! I crowned you, I rewarded you,
> And all the time you were cheating on the side.

PAPHLAGON.

> All right, I cheated – for the city's sake.

DEMOS.

> Take off that crown. It belongs to him, not you.

AGORAKRITOS.

> Go on. Take off my crown, you heap of dung.

PAPHLAGON.

> No, I won't. I've still another oracle.
1230 > Only one man on Earth can do me down.

AGORAKRITOS.

> That's right: me. You can't wriggle out of it.

PAPHLAGON.

> Oh, yes I can. Just answer this questionnaire,
> And see if you fit the bill. Question One:
> Where were you born? Where did you go to school?

AGORAKRITOS.

> Born in the gutter, knocked into shape in the
>   cookhouse.

PAPHLAGON (*aside, overacting*).

> Exactly as the oracle describes!

> (*to* AGORAKRITOS)

> All right: what training did you get at school?

AGORAKRITOS.

> Stealing and lying and saying it was someone else.

PAPHLAGON (*aside, as before*).

> Apollo! What are you trying to do to me?   1240

(*to* AGORAKRITOS)

Question Three: what did you do when you grew up?

AGORAKRITOS.
I peddled tripe, and –

PAPHLAGON.
Well?

AGORAKRITOS.
Ooh, sailor, can't you guess?

PAPHLAGON (*aside, as before*).
Another blow! The gods are on to me.
There's only one chance left, one little chance.

(*to* AGORAKRITOS)

Last question: did you have a proper stall
In the market, or a trolley in the docks?

AGORAKRITOS.
In the docks, of course. By the herring-stand.

PAPHLAGON.
Oh no! The oracle's come true! The gods
Have wrapped me up and done me down. My crown,   1250
My darling crown, the time has come: farewell.
Into someone else's hands, a luckier man,
But never, never, a bigger crook than me.

He breaks down.

AGORAKRITOS.
Well, thank you, Zeus. You helped me win.

CHORUS.
We helped you win. Especially me. Look here,
Old boy...my lord, my hero, my conqueror...
Got any jobs for the boys? The old school tie...?
I mean, I scratched your back – now you scratch
   mine.

DEMOS.
My dear boy, my hero, what's your name?

AGORAKRITOS.
Agorakritos.

(*to the audience*)

That means Common Man. Common as muck...

DEMOS.
Agorakritos, I'm yours. Look after me.
And *this* is yours as well. Look after it.   1260

AGORAKRITOS.
Oh, thank you, master. I'll see to you, all right.
I'll look after you like no one else, ever.
I'll clean up this city of...bloody fools.

He leads DEMOS *inside. Exit* PAPHLAGON.

CHORUS.
It's always nice, in plays,
To put in a little praise
Of galloping horsemen, proud and quick –
But *not* Thoumantis. He makes me sick.
1270   He's always hungry, praying at Apollo's shrine
In floods of tears, with a pitiful whine,
For a crust of bread, for a scrap of meat.
For *something* to eat.

Ariphrades! That swine!
Who?
Ariphrades.
Never heard of him?
Arignotos' brother. Yes,
Good old Arignotos. One of the best.
1280   So what's wrong with his brother?
You mean you haven't heard? Some are born vile,
Some have vileness thrust upon them –
But he *invented* vileness. Thrives on it.
Just listen to him playing the flute,
Then think of the whores that mouth has blown,
Just imagine that filthy, acrobatic tongue –

And if *that* doesn't turn your stomach,
Don't imagine you'll ever get a drink from me.

I sit up half the night   1290
And fret. I wrestle and fight
And rack my brains. I toss about
And try to work the answer out.
It's a problem, a puzzle to end all puzzles.
Where does Kleonymos put the food he guzzles?
He's like an ostrich: I think he'd be able
To eat the table.

Have you heard the latest?
What?
The warships   1300
Got together for a gossip.
The oldest whoreship, the madam, said,
'Know what's happening, girls?
He wants to send a hundred of us out
To Africa. Who? Old vinegar-puss Hyperbolos,
That's who.' You should have heard the fuss.
One of them (young, never shipped a man) said,
'He won't spread *my* sail! I'd rather rot.'
Another said, 'It's rape, not business, girls.   1310
Let's sail to the Akropolis for sanctuary.
He won't lead Athens up the garden path –
Let him launch one of his lamps, and sail to Hell!'

Fanfares. AGORAKRITOS *comes out.*

AGORAKRITOS.
   Gather round, shut your faces, clap your hands.
   Close the courts and start the holiday.
   It's happy time. The day of days has dawned.

CHORUS.
   O morning star, dayspring of joy, what news?
   What miracle, to set our hearts on fire?   1320

AGORAKRITOS.
   I've been stewing old Demos, inside.
   I've restored him. I've brought back his youth.

CHORUS.
What a miracle! Where is he now?

AGORAKRITOS.
Here, in fabulous Athens. Where else?

CHORUS.
And he's really been changed? What's he like?

AGORAKRITOS.
Like he was before, in the good old days.
Look: he's coming. They're opening the doors.
Raise a cheer, now, for Athens restored
To the glory and greatness of old.

More fanfares. Enter DEMOS *in state,
dressed in gorgeous robes and carrying a
sceptre topped with a gold cicada.*

CHORUS.
Sing, Athens, the glittering, violet-crowned,
1330   The envy of the world. Your prince has come.

AGORAKRITOS.
Himself is here. The Great Big Boss, at last,
With his robes in the old-fashioned style
And his golden cicada of state.
No more law-courts, just parties and peace.

CHORUS.
Hail, prince of the Greeks. Please accept
Our congratulations on this worthy change
Back to the old style, which made us great.

DEMOS.
Hey, Aggie, come here. Aren't you clever?
That boiling really did me a power of good.

AGORAKRITOS.
Of course it did. Just think how you've changed,
Just think what you were like before,
And you'll call me a god.

DEMOS.

What d'you mean, what I was like before?

AGORAKRITOS.

Don't you remember? The Assembly, for a start.   1340
All you needed was someone to say,
'I love you, Demos. O People, be mine,
Mine alone. Let me look after you, for evermore'...
Soft soap like that, and you were away,
Flapping your wings, crowing, preening yourself –

DEMOS.

Was I?

AGORAKRITOS.

Yes. They had you right where they wanted you.

DEMOS.

So they did. And I never felt a thing.

AGORAKRITOS.

They had your ears in the palm of their hand.
Open, shut...open, shut...just like folding doors.

DEMOS.

I must have been crazy, or doddering.

AGORAKRITOS.

Remember the row there was over that money?   1350
Whether it should be used to build more ships
Or to give public officials a rise in pay?
The pay-man came in first. The ships nowhere.
Now what's the matter? What are you wriggling for?

DEMOS.

I'm ashamed. I was such a fool before.

AGORAKRITOS.

No, no, no. It wasn't your fault. It was them:
Them liars and cheats. Things are different now.
Suppose some bully of a lawyer said
'Find the prisoner guilty, or you get no pay' –   1360
What would you do to him now? The lawyer, I mean.

DEMOS.

> I'd throw him over the nearest cliff – and chuck
> Hyperbolos on top of him.

AGORAKRITOS.

> There you are, you see.
> Now, what's your policy for government?

DEMOS.

> First, when the warships next put into port,
> I'll see that every sailor gets his pay.

AGORAKRITOS.

> That'll make every calloused bottom smile.

DEMOS.

> And once a man's name's on the army roll,
> It'll stay there, despite his fancy friends.
> No more transfers. No buying a passage home.

AGORAKRITOS.

> Poor Kleonymos! Another loophole closed.

DEMOS.

> There'll be no more lounging outside barber's
>   shops.

AGORAKRITOS.

> Ooh! Kleisthenes and Straton... Aren't you *butch?*

DEMOS.

> No, no, not them. Them intellectuals,
> I mean, with nothing else to do but talk.
> 'Take Phaiax, now. Such style, such eloquence!
> Such *density*...such *poise*...such *irony*...'
> And such a way with those who interrupt...

AGORAKRITOS.

> Oh, that lot. Two fingers for them, O.K.?

DEMOS.

> No, better than that: I'll make them learn to *hunt.*

1370 *(line number, margin)*

1380 *(line number, margin)*

AGORAKRITOS.

Good. You'll need this deckchair then. And this boy...
This ballsy boy...to carry it. Put it up any time you
like.

DEMOS.

The good old days are back again.

AGORAKRITOS.

Not half. Just wait till you see what else I've got.

He brings in two GIRLS.

There you are. They're peace-treaties. All for you.

DEMOS.

Peace-treaties, eh? I'll see they're ratified.   1390
Very nice...very nice. Where did you pick *them* up?

AGORAKRITOS.

Paphlagon had them hidden away, inside,
So you could never get your hands on them.
But now they're yours. A present from me.
Take them home with you to the countryside.

DEMOS.

And what about Paphlagon? What punishment
Have you in store for him?

AGORAKRITOS.

Punishment, nothing.
He can have my tripe-stall, down in the docks.
Sell dog-meat and horse-meat, all on his own.
He can get drunk, and argue with the whores...   1400
And whenever he likes, he can take a running jump...

DEMOS.

Brilliant! Whores...take a running jump...
Just what he's fit for. Just what he deserves.
Now then, you come inside with me,
To dinner. You can have his place. It's yours.
Put on this dinner-jacket, and follow me.
The rest of you, deliver Paphlagon

To his sausage-stall, where all his friends,
All his victims, can go and laugh at him.

Exeunt omnes.

PEACE

Characters

TRYGAIOS
TRYGAIOS' TWO SLAVES
TRYGAIOS' ELDEST CHILD
HERMES
WAR
QUARREL
HIEROKLES
SICKLE-MAKER
ARMOURER
TWO BOYS

silent parts:

TRYGAIOS' YOUNGER CHILDREN
CITIZEN
COMMANDOS
DUNG-BEETLE
ARMOURER'S FRIENDS
HARVEST
HOLIDAY
LAMACHOS
PEACE (a statue)
SHEEP

CHORUS OF FARMERS

On one side, the door of TRYGAIOS' *farmhouse. Beside it, a stable door. On the other side of the stage, the doorway to Heaven. Centre back, a cave-mouth, blocked by boulders.* TRYGAIOS' *door is flung open, and the* FIRST SLAVE *comes out.*

FIRST SLAVE.
  Come on! It's feeding time. Bring out the beetle's lunch.

The SECOND SLAVE *comes out with a bucket.*

SECOND SLAVE.
  Here.

FIRST SLAVE.
  You feed the bastard. And tell him from me
  I hope he chokes.

  The SECOND SLAVE *empties his bucket into the stable.*

FIRST SLAVE.
  Now give him another one. Ass-dung this time.

SECOND SLAVE.
  There.

FIRST SLAVE.
  What's happened to the first one? Has he eaten it?

SECOND SLAVE.
  It's hardly *eating*, is it? Jump, roll, squeeze –
  You know the way he works.

FIRST SLAVE.
  So, *jump* inside
  And *squeeze* some more. Fat...juicy...thick...

SECOND SLAVE (*to the audience*).
  For gawd's sake, bog-attendants, come and help.
  D'you want to see me drowning in the stuff?   10

FIRST SLAVE.
  Quick! Give him another. That little one,
  That pansy pie. He likes a bit of mince[19].

SECOND SLAVE.
  There.

Look for the silver lining, I always say:
Feed *him*, and diet – I wanted to lose some weight.

FIRST SLAVE (*passing a bucket*).
Here! Quick! Get back on line.

SECOND SLAVE (*passing it back*).
I'm up to here with it.

FIRST SLAVE.
Take it!

SECOND SLAVE.
You take it, and go to Hell!

The FIRST SLAVE *takes the bucket into the
stable. The* SECOND SLAVE *addresses the audience.*

20   Ladies and gentlemen. Wanted – a nose
Without a pair of holes. It's serious.
Playing pat-a-cake with beetle-food's no fun.
A pig or a dog, now: drop it where you like,
They lap it up. No fuss. But not Lord Muck:
He sticks his nose in the air, won't touch a bite
Unless I spend the whole day working it,
Kneading it, patting it into perfect balls.
Balls! Who does he think he is?
It's gone very quiet. I'd better take a look.

He opens the stable door.

30   Easy does it...not too wide...

He recoils.

That's right, don't stop. Keep guzzling till you
    burst.

(*to the audience*)

He eats like a wrestling match:
Head down, shoulders pumping, chomping jaws,
Lots of little legs going in and out –
You'd think he was plaiting anchor-ropes.

The FIRST SLAVE *comes out of the stable.*

FIRST SLAVE.
  Bastard! Filthy brute!

SECOND SLAVE.
  Which god d'you think looks after him?

FIRST SLAVE.
  What?

SECOND SLAVE.
  Aphrodite, goddess of beauty? Nah.   40
  The Graces? Nah.

FIRST SLAVE.
  Well, who?

SECOND SLAVE.
  Zeus, lord of the thunder-crap.

  (*to the audience*)

  Hands up who understands what's going on.
  Sonny Jim over there? He thinks
  He knows everything. No, he's whispering
  To his neighbour, 'Why the beetle? What's the point?'
  'It's satire, see. Political. They're all
  Shit-eaters in politics – and so is he.'

FIRST SLAVE.
  I've got to go in. The beetle needs a drink.

  He goes in.

SECOND SLAVE.
  Now we're alone, I'll tell you lot the plot.
  Can you hear me at the front...?   50
  In the middle...?
  AT THE BACK...?
  My master's round the bend. Not mad like you,
  Not *normal* craziness. This is something else.
  He stands all day like this, looking up at the sky
  With his mouth open, shouting at the gods.

'Oi! Zeus!' he shouts. 'What's up? What's eating
    you?
Put down your broom. Don't brush us off just yet.'

TRYGAIOS (*inside*).
    Ee-ah! Eee-aaah!

SECOND SLAVE.
60   Shut up a minute. I think I heard a voice.

TRYGAIOS (*inside*).
    Zeus, Zeus, what hast thou in mind for us?
    Thou drain'st us, yea, squeezest our very pips.

SECOND SLAVE.
    Told you. His very words. And that's not all.
    Just hear what he said when he first went mad.
    'Suppose' (he said) 'Suppose I go myself,
    All the way up to Heaven, and have a word
    With Zeus in person?' He fetched a pair of steps
70   And startled climbing them. To heaven! *Fell?*
    Of course he fell. He nearly broke his neck.
    So then he disappeared, and came back with *this* –
    This thoroughbred beetle bastard.
    He strokes it, cuddles it and whispers in its ear,
    'My Pegasos! My noble, wingéd steed,
    Who'll fly me to Zeus with grace and speed – '
    You know the lines. You saw that tragedy.
    Just a minute. He's in there now. What's he doing?
    Oh god! Help! Neighbours! Help!
80   He's off! Halfway to Heaven, on beetle-back!

TRYGAIOS *rides out of the stable on a huge prop*
DUNG-BEETLE, *attached to the theatre crane.*

TRYGAIOS.
    Gently now, gently now, steady there, whoa boy!
    Stop strutting and prancing –
    Stop dancing!
    Harvest your energy,
    Harness it tight
    Till you zoom into take-off

And soar into flight.
And for god's sake don't fart
Before we start.

SECOND SLAVE.
Look, master, you're potty.   90

TRYGAIOS.
Shut up. Get down.

SECOND SLAVE.
Sky-riding's dotty!

TRYGAIOS.
After long deliberation
And careful preparation
I take to the air – for Greece.

SECOND SLAVE.
Don't be daft. Come down.

TRYGAIOS.
Smile and cheer.
Don't jeer.
Take this message to the human race:
'Brick up your privies. Bung your bums – '   100

SECOND SLAVE.
I refuse to brick or bung
Till you tell me where you're going.

TRYGAIOS.
To Zeus in Heaven, of course.

SECOND SLAVE.
What for?

TRYGAIOS.
To ask what he has in store for Greece.

SECOND SLAVE.
Suppose he won't answer?

TRYGAIOS.
I've ways of making him. He'll talk.

SECOND SLAVE.
Over my dead body!

TRYGAIOS.
Get out of the way!

SECOND SLAVE.
110   Hoo! Hoo! Hoo!
Help! Children! Your Daddy's sneaking off
To Heaven and leaving you. Come out, come out,
Poor mites, and beg your Dad to stay.

Enter CHILDREN.

CHILD.
O Daddy, Daddy, was it true,
The tale they told? Absurd!
You've got to fly! How can you – *you?*
You're not a bird.
Oh Daddy, Daddy, tell me it's not true.

TRYGAIOS.
Children...children...my mind's made up. How can
I bear
120   To see your little faces asking for bread
When there's nothing in the cupboard at all...
at all?
If this plan works, if I get back alive,
You'll each get a bun – and a clip on the ear as
well!

CHILD.
But how will you get to Heaven, Dad?
No ferry-boats there are, no ships.

TRYGAIOS
Who needs ships? I've got my wingéd steed.

CHILD.
You've lost your marbles! How
Can *that* thing take you up to Heav'n?

TRYGAIOS.
Like in that Aesop fable. 'Once upon
A time, a beetle flew to Heav'n' –   130

CHILD.
Oh Daddy, dear!
A smelly thing like that?

TRYGAIOS.
The story says,
When Zeus' eagle stole its babies, up
It flew and snitched the eagle's eggs.

CHILD.
You ought to use a wingéd horse
Like Pegasos. More dignified.

TRYGAIOS.
Look, wingéd horses need to eat.
The extra food means extra weight.
With *him*, *I* eat – and feed him later on.

CHILD.
What if you tumble in the stormy brine?   140
How can a wingéd beetle save you then?

TRYGAIOS.
I've got my punt-pole ready.
He's the boat.

CHILD.
What port will take thee, wand'ring, in?

TRYGAIOS.
Piraeus. They'll take in anyone.

CHILD.
Take care, in case you slip and fall
And give Euripides the theme
For yet another limping tragedy.

TRYGAIOS.
Yes, anything but that. But it's time to go.
Ladies and gentlemen, all this hard work   150

Is for *your* sakes. What can *you* do for me?
Simple. For the next three days don't shit or fart –
For if he gets wind of it from up on high
He'll throw me off and dive back down for lunch.
Gee up now, Pegasos, prance away;
Prick up your ears to the golden chink
Of bit and bridle. On we go!

The BEETLE *begins to rise into the air. Its*
flight is none too steady.

Hey! What are you doing? Don't
Divert your nose to the public bogs.
Will yourself up from Earth,
160   Spread your wings, and fly
Straight as an arrow to the court of Zeus.
Absent thee from felicity awhile,
Put off the droppings of mortality.
Hey! You! What are you doing
Shitting beside that whore-house in Piraeus?
You'll be the death of me. Dig a hole
And bury it. Pile up a funeral mound,
Drop rose-petals,
Sprinkle scent. If I
170   End up in the shit, you'll be sorry –
Damages, arse-tronomical,
Because of one unruly bum.
Oh dear! I'm not enjoying this. Hey,
You on the crane, keep your mind on the job.
My guts are knotted up with wind –
Another lurch, and I'll give the beetle lunch.

The BEETLE *comes to rest outside the door*
of Heaven.

Aha! This looks like Zeus' place. Whoa, boy!

He gets off and knocks.

Hello! Open up! Is anyone at home?

HERMES *opens the door.*

HERMES.
  Do I smell mortal?   180
  Zeus guard us all, what's that?

TRYGAIOS.
  What's it look like? A hippokantharos.

HERMES.
  You bare-faced bastard! Cheeky swine!
  You stinking so-and-so, you dirty rat,
  What brings you here? And what's your name?

TRYGAIOS.
  So-and-so.

HERMES.
  First name?

TRYGAIOS.
  So-and-so.

HERMES.
  Father's name?

TRYGAIOS.
  So-and-so.

HERMES.
  By Earth, you're dead unless I hear your name.

TRYGAIOS.
  Trygaios, from Athmonia near Athens.   190
  A farmer, a wine-grower.
  I love my country and hate all politics.

HERMES.
  But why come here?

TRYGAIOS.
  I've brought you something. *This*.

HERMES.
  My *dear!* What can I do for you?

TRYGAIOS.
  Hey, times have changed.

What happened to So-and-so?
Never mind. Call Zeus.

HERMES.
Ha! Zeus! You won't get near the gods. They've
    gone.
Packed all their luggage yesterday, and moved.

TRYGAIOS.
But where on Earth – ?

HERMES.
Don't make me laugh. On Earth?

TRYGAIOS.
Well, where then?

HERMES.
Miles from here.
They're in...the foreskin of the sky.

TRYGAIOS.
200   But why are you still here, all on your own?

HERMES.
Well, someone had to stay, to keep an eye
On the crockery, the cutlery, the pots and pans...

TRYGAIOS.
What made them move so suddenly?

HERMES.
You Greeks.
They've had you up to *here*. They've leased this place
To War, left him to sort you out. They've gone
As far away as possible – they don't want to watch
Your squabbling any more, or hear your prayers.

TRYGAIOS.
210   But what have we *done*? Why turn on us?

HERMES.
War-mania. You're mad for it. Whenever Heaven
Comes up with a plan for peace, you veto it.
When the Spartans gain an inch, they say,

'Up yours' to Athens – and if *you*
Have a little bit of luck, and the Spartans ask for peace,
You say, 'Total victory. Get knotted.'

TRYGAIOS.

You've caught the tone of voice.   220

HERMES.

The upshot is, you won't see Peace again.

TRYGAIOS.

Don't tell me she's gone too.

HERMES.

War's thrown her in
A black abyss.

TRYGAIOS.

A what?

HERMES.

A black abyss.
That one, there. Those huge great stones are there
To block the entrance. You'll never dig her out.

TRYGAIOS.

What about us? Has he something else in store?

HERMES.

All I know is, when he arrived last night
He had a vast great anvil with him[20].

TRYGAIOS.

An anvil? Whatever for?   230

HERMES.

To pound the Greeks on – what d'you think?

Noise off-stage.

I think he's coming out. Did you hear
That clattering? I'm off.

He goes in.

TRYGAIOS.
Oo-er! I hear the anvil chorus too.

He hides. Enter WAR, *with an anvil.*

WAR.
Yoh mortals, mortals, mortals! Pain,
Tooth-grinding agony. Yoh woe! Yoh woe!

TRYGAIOS (*aside*).
Apollo, what an anvil. Don't tell me *he's*

240   The one we're frightened of? We shit our pants
For *him* – this fairground freak, this Big Bad Wolf?

WAR.
Yoh Prasians! Thrice-wretched! Five-fold,
Ten-fold misery! This plough's for you.

TRYGAIOS (*aside*).
A plough for Prasiai? Huh! So what if they
Get furrowed? They're Sparta's friends, not ours.

WAR.
Yoh Megara, Megara! Topple and quail!
This mattock will mash you to mindless mince.

TRYGAIOS (*aside*).
A mashing for Megara? Messy.

WAR.
Yoh Sicily! You'll be slashed and sliced.

TRYGAIOS (*aside*).
250   How sickening for Sicily.

WAR.
Now, arrows for Athens.

TRYGAIOS (*aside*).
Arrows for Athens? How harrowing.
We're such a sitting target.

WAR.
Quarrel! Quarrel! Where's that boy?

Enter QUARREL.

QUARREL.
  You called?

WAR.
  Don't take that tone with me. Don't dawdle. Here!

QUARREL.
  Ow! What have you got in there,
  A bag of nails?

WAR.
  Where's the hammer?

QUARREL.
  There isn't a hammer.
  We only moved in yesterday.   260

WAR.
  Fetch one from Athens, idiot. And fetch it quick.

QUARREL.
  All right, all right. No need to shout.

  Exit.

TRYGAIOS (*aside*).
  Oh dear!
  Things don't look good.
  If he brings a hammer, we've had it.
  War'll pound us to little bits.
  Pray for an accident – going down or coming up.

  Enter QUARREL.

WAR.
  Well?

QUARREL.
  Well, what?

WAR.
  Where's the hammer?

QUARREL.
  There isn't one.
  They had one in Athens once,

270   General Kleon, Hammer of Greece –
    But now he's dead.

TRYGAIOS (*aside*).
    Thank god for that.
    I always said if you gave Kleon time,
    He was bound to do *something* right.

WAR.
    Don't just stand there. Go to Sparta. Now!

QUARREL.
    Sparta. Right.

    Exit.

TRYGAIOS (*aside*).
    Ladies and gentlemen, I should shut your eyes.
    Forget the accident – we need a miracle.

    Enter QUARREL.

QUARREL.
280   Oh, hoo hoo hoo! Hoo hoo!

WAR.
    What now? Where is it? Well?

QUARREL.
    Their hammer's gone as well.

WAR.
    You little... *What* did you say?

QUARREL.
    General Brasidas. They lent him out,
    And never got him back.
    You know what it's like when you lend your tools.

TRYGAIOS (*aside*).
    We *got* a miracle.
    You can open your eyes – things are looking up.

WAR.
    All right. Bring all the stuff inside.
    I'll *make* a hammer. Hurry up!

Exeunt WAR *and* QUARREL. TRYGAIOS *comes out.*

TRYGAIOS.
Yahoo! Yay! Wow! Ya-yoh! Ya-yoh! –
As milady said when she got the part[21].   290
This is our chance. Let's pull together now
And rescue lovely Peace before he gets back.
Let's spring-clean Greece,
Let's wipe the floor with War.
Come up and help,
Farmers, shopkeepers, carpenters,
Road-menders, immigrants, emigrants, islanders.
Bring shovels, crowbars, ropes.
We've got our hands on luck at last –
Let's grab it and haul it in.   300

Enter CHORUS.

CHORUS.
This way! Dance down salvation's road.
Dance to the rescue, Greeks, unite and dance.
Forget route-marches, army cloaks.
The day of happiness has dawned.
Great architect of peace, what next?
We're ready. We'll never tire. We'll heave
And pull and haul; we'll bring to light
Her smiling majesty, lady of the vine.

TRYGAIOS.
Shh! Shh! Calm down. D'you want
War blazing up again, like a forest fire?   310

CHORUS.
We heard the trumpet-call for happiness.
We heard; we're here.

TRYGAIOS.
Keep dancing and singing, you'll wake the dead –
Yes, *him*, Kleon, watchdog of the state.
He'll fume and foam and bag her back again.

CHORUS.
No one alive or dead will bag her back
Once *we* get hold of her. Ee-oo! Ee-oo!

They dance.

TRYGAIOS.
Be quiet! You'll blow it! *He'll* come roaring out,
All fists and feet, and pulp us.

CHORUS.
320   So let him fist and feet and pulp – who cares?
We're dancing, and we don't intend to stop.

TRYGAIOS.
You're crazy! You're raving mad! We'd a chance
In a million – and you're dancing it away.

CHORUS.
It's not us dancing. It's our legs.
They're jumping for joy. They can't control
    themselves.

TRYGAIOS.
Save jumping for later. For god's sake, STOP!

CHORUS.
330   We're stopping. Look.

TRYGAIOS.
You're nothing of the kind.

CHORUS.
Just eight more bars. We promise. Then we'll stop.

TRYGAIOS.
Eight bars, and then you stop for good.

CHORUS.
You only had to ask.

TRYGAIOS (*after a moment*).
You've not stopped yet.

CHORUS.
Just one more step, and...STOP!

The dance abruptly stops.

We'll have to do eight more, to straighten up.

TRYGAIOS.
Go on then, eight more bars.

The dance resumes.

CHORUS.
Who laughs and shouts for joy?
Who farts and sings?
All those who shed their shields
And spread their wings.

TRYGAIOS.
It isn't wing-time yet. When Peace is ours
You can laugh and shout,
Dance in and out,   340
Go cruising, stay,
Go boozing, play;
You can fuck (with luck),
Have forty drinks –
You can take your ease,
Do what you please –
BUT NOT TILL PEACE IS OURS.

CHORUS.
God send it soon.
What a time we've had!
Route-marches, bivouacs,
Left, right, left, right, aching feet,   350
Spears, shields, day in, day out.
Things will be different now.
We'll shed war's camouflage:
Leather faces, sandpaper eyes
Will relax and smile.

The dance ends.

All right, we're ready. What would you like us to do?
You're the boss, you're our lucky charm. Speak up.   360

TRYGAIOS.
The first problem is how to shift those rocks.

Enter HERMES.

HERMES.
Swine! So-and-so! What are you up to now?

TRYGAIOS.
Nothing. Don't panic. It's quite all right.

HERMES.
You're dead!

TRYGAIOS.
Pardon?

HERMES.
Wiped out, deceased.

TRYGAIOS.
When?

HERMES.
Now.

TRYGAIOS.
370   Never felt a thing.

HERMES.
March!

TRYGAIOS.
No thanks.

HERMES.
But didn't you hear what Zeus decreed?
'Who diggeth, dieth.'

TRYGAIOS.
Diggeth?

HERMES.
Dieth.

TRYGAIOS.
But I haven't packed my lunch.

HERMES.
Thundering Zeus!

TRYGAIOS.
No! Please don't tell!

HERMES.
I will if I want.

TRYGAIOS.
I brought you sausages.

HERMES.
My dear, be reasonable. I'm only doing my job.   380
'Lift up your voice,' he said, 'or bite the dust.'

TRYGAIOS.
Hold on. Don't lift it yet.

(*to the* CHORUS)

Well, don't just stand there. You heard:
He's going to lift his voice. Speak up!

CHORUS.
No, no, no, no!
Think of the peace-time pigs
We sacrificed – the pork,
The crackling, for your delight.
You said yes then; don't say no now.

TRYGAIOS.
Look how they're grovelling. Smile.

CHORUS.
Don't turn away. Don't frown.   390
Benefactor!
Philanthropist!
Help us rescue Peace.
Oh, think about it, lord.
No more bristling eyebrows...
Processions all day long...

TRYGAIOS.
Lord Hermes, hear

Their supplication.

400 *Please.*
They've never shown respect like this before.

HERMES.
Never scrounged like this before.

TRYGAIOS.
I'll tell you a monster plot
Being hatched against the gods, right now.

HERMES.
Go on. I promise nothing, mind.

TRYGAIOS.
The Moon and that cheating swine the Sun
Have been plotting together for ages now
To hand Greece over to...the Primitives.

HERMES.
I'm still listening.

TRYGAIOS.
The point is, the Primitives
410 Worship the Sun and Moon, but in civilised Greece
We sacrifice to *you*. The Olympians. So if
The Sun and Moon get rid of us, *they* get
The offerings, and *you* get nothing.

HERMES.
I *thought* the days were getting shorter.

TRYGAIOS.
Exactly. Your only chance is to help us now.
Lend a hand with Peace, and you'll be king:
Place of honour at feasts and festivals,
Special mention at every sacrifice.
'Hermes the Liberator' – your name will be   420
On every pair of lips in Greece. Besides,
There's something else. I've brought you a little
    gift.

He produces a golden drinking-cup.

HERMES.
Ooh! I go all trembly at the glimpse of gold.
All right. Take one of those crowbars each
And lever away the stones.

CHORUS.
Wisest of gods, at once.
You're the boss. We'll do exactly as you say.   430

During what follows, some of the CHORUS
remove the stones blocking the cave-mouth,
and lay out ropes.

TRYGAIOS.
Hold out the cup. We'll pour an offering
And say a prayer before we start.

HERMES.
Keep silence. Keep silence
While we make this offering.

TRYGAIOS.
May happiness dawn in Greece today.
May everyone who pulls these ropes
Never lay hands again on shield or spear.

CHORUS.
May they live all their days in peace,
With loved ones to cuddle and a fire to poke.   440

TRYGAIOS.
All those who say, 'Make war, not love' –

CHORUS.
May they fish arrows from their funny-bone.

TRYGAIOS.
If any would-be general frowns at Peace –

CHORUS.
May he turn into Kleonymos and shed his shield.

TRYGAIOS.
  If any spear-supplier opposes us –

CHORUS.
  Out of his bottom may the market fall.

TRYGAIOS.
450 All those too slack to pull their weight –

CHORUS.
  May they be smashed, and wheeled, and
  dumped.

TRYGAIOS.
  Send *us* good luck.

CHORUS.
  You can't beat that.

TRYGAIOS.
  Forget the beating. Just 'amen'.

CHORUS.
  Forget the beating. Just 'amen'.

TRYGAIOS.
  Now, pour the offering.
  To Hermes, the Graces, Beauty, Love, Desire –

HERMES.
  War?

TRYGAIOS.
  No.

HERMES.
  No battle-gods?

TRYGAIOS.
  None.
  Now, everyone take hold. Let's haul them in.

  The CHORUS-*men stand in lines, facing the
  audience, with ropes over their shoulders –
  as if preparing to haul a boat inshore.*

HERMES.
Heave ho.

CHORUS.
Heave.   460

HERMES.
Heave ho.

CHORUS.
Heave.

TRYGAIOS.
Just a minute. They're not all pulling.
One more effort. One single pan-Hellenic pull.
That means you Thebans too.

*They take up their positions again. But
a group of* COMMANDOS *has come in, and now
prepares to pull in the opposite direction.*

HERMES.
Right? Heave ho.

TRYGAIOS.
Heave.

CHORUS.
Why don't you two pull as well?

TRYGAIOS.
I'm pulling, panting sweat.
What more d'you want?

CHORUS.
We're getting nowhere. Why?

TRYGAIOS.
It's Lamachos. Get out of it!   470
Who invited *you?* Don't wave that thing at me.

He shoos them out.

HERMES.
The Mycenaeans aren't helping much.

TRYGAIOS.
They've fattened on neutrality for years.
Help both, help neither – it's all the same to them.

HERMES.
The Spartans are doing their share.

TRYGAIOS.
Especially our prisoners. *They* want peace, all right.
480   They'd pull still harder if they weren't in chains.

HERMES.
The Megarians here are getting down to it.
Tugging, kicking, biting.

TRYGAIOS.
What d'you expect?
They haven't had a decent meal for years.

CHORUS.
Never mind the satire. Get on with it.
All it needs is for everyone to pull.

HERMES.
Heave ho.

CHORUS
Heave.

HERMES.
Heave ho.

CHORUS.
Heave.

TRYGAIOS.
490   It's hardly moving. It's ridiculous.
Some are *still* hanging back. Come *on*!
Get it sorted *out*!

HERMES.
Right? Heave ho.

TRYGAIOS.
Heave.

CHORUS.
We're still getting nowhere.

TRYGAIOS.
Harder! Don't you want to get
Your hands on Peace?

CHORUS.
There's someone slowing us down.

TRYGAIOS.
It's this lot here.   500
They've done nothing but argue since they came.
Good heavens, they're Athenians! All talk,
No action. Look: d'you really want to help?
You do? Stop telling us how – just pull.

CHORUS.
Come on, farmers. We'll do the job ourselves.

HERMES.
It's coming.

TRYGAIOS.
He says it's coming. Heave.   510

CHORUS.
I told you: leave it to the farmers.
Heave ho. Heave.

HERMES.
A little more...

CHORUS.
Pull harder! Pull!

HERMES.
Nearly there.

CHORUS.
Heave ho. Heave.
Heave ho. Heave ho. Heave.
Heave ho. Heave ho. Heave ho. HEAVE.

PEACE, a statue, is pulled out of the cave-mouth
to the position it will hold until the end of the
play. With it are two beautiful, live attendants,
HARVEST *and* HOLIDAY.

TRYGAIOS.
520   Mistress, giver of grapes, what can I say?
    What ten-thousand-wine-cask word, to welcome
        you?
    Oh Harvest...Holiday...

He kisses HARVEST, HOLIDAY, *and then the statue.*

    Oh lady, your lips!
    Your breath gentles my heart.
    I smell forget-me-nots, forget-to-fight –

HERMES.
    No kitbags?

TRYGAIOS.
    Don't talk of kitbags now. A kitbag smells
    Of gut-rot.

HERMES.
    Cheese-and-onion –

TRYGAIOS.
    Feet.
530   She smells of vineyards –

HERMES.
    Parties –

TRYGAIOS.
    The good old songs –

HERMES.
    Euripides?

TRYGAIOS.
    Why should she smell of *that*
    Poetic mincing-machine?
    She smells of ivy wreaths –

HERMES.
Wine-strainers –

TRYGAIOS.
Bleating sheep –

HERMES.
Barmaids –

TRYGAIOS.
Tipsy slaves –

HERMES.
Wine-cups –

TRYGAIOS.
Happiness, oh happiness!

HERMES (*pointing to the* CHORUS).
They're happy, for a start:
Laughing, joking, all good friends again.

TRYGAIOS.
What's a black eye or two between good friends?   540

HERMES.
And look at the audience. You can tell
By the faces they're making what each one does.

TRYGAIOS.
What about that one, tearing his hair?

HERMES.
He makes horsehair crests.

TRYGAIOS.
He makes windmills. Look: he's making wind
At his neighbour the sword-seller.

HERMES.
He makes pitchforks – he's certainly got stuck in,
Forking that corporal in the next-door seat.

TRYGAIOS (*to the audience*).
It's clever, isn't it?

HERMES.
  It's time
550   To demobilise the farmers, and send them home.

TRYGAIOS (*to the* CHORUS).
  Listen. An announcement. ALL COUNTRY FOLK
  ARE HEREBY FREE TO FARM THEIR LAND IN
    PEACE.
  SPEARS, SWORDS AND JAVELINS WILL BE
    EXCHANGED
  FOR IMPLEMENTS OF AGRICULTURE. PEACE
  IS DECLARED IN SEASON. NOW. AT ONCE.
    BY LAW.
  Sing her a hymn of thanks, and be on your way.

CHORUS.
  Dayspring of joy,
  Delight of all farmers,
  How I longed for you; how I longed
  To say hello to the vines, the figs
  I planted in the good old days
  So long, so long ago.

TRYGAIOS.
560   Sing thanks; throw crests and shields away.
  Pack sandwiches; we're homeward bound.
  Fields! Farms! Homeward bound at last.

HERMES.
  Poseidon, what a pretty sight. Neat, trim,
  Manly, faces shining like sugar-buns.

TRYGAIOS.
  Forks ready, hoes clean and sharp –
  I can hardly wait.
  What a treat for our furrows –
570   I want to get home, and dig.
  Oh my friends, do you remember
  The life we led,
  The days of Peace?
  Rose-petals, raisins, figs,

Sweet grape-juice,
Honey-cakes,
Violet-beds beside the well,
Olive groves – oh, sing to her,   580
Remember happiness and sing.

CHORUS.
Welcome, dearest.
What a time we've had!
Worn with longing,
Gnawed by hope –
Would happiness come back?
Would Peace
Fill our thirsty fields with joy?   590
We suffered,
And then you came:
Salvation, rich and full.
Our vines,
Our green figs
Smile to greet you;
Our shoots hold out their arms.

TRYGAIOS.
But what made her stay away so long?   600
Kindest of gods, can you tell us that?

HERMES.
Friends, neighbours, countrymen, pin back your ears.
I'll tell you exactly what pissed her off.
It began with that statue in the Parthenon.
Pallas Athene. Pheidias fiddled his accounts,
And you banished him. That panicked Perikles:
He saw your teeth, and wondered if he'd be next.
You needed a smoke-screen to take your minds
Off political accounts. So he started a fire
With a little decree forbidding trade with Megara.
Smoke-screen! Eyes watered all over Greece.   610
Vines withered in the flames; pots cracked;
No one could put it out – *she* pined away.

TRYGAIOS (*aside to the* CHORUS LEADER).
Who'd have thought that Peace
Had anything to do with Pheidias?

CHORUS (*aside to him*).
I suppose, if you're a statue,
It pays to have a sculptor up your sleeve.

HERMES.
When your allies saw you snarling and baring your
620   teeth,
They took their cue from you. A bribe or two
In Sparta (top politicians there the same as here:
Fond of money, not fond of strangers), and that
    was that –
Peace out on her ear, War grabbed with greedy
    hands.
That was fine for the city, but not for country folk:
Athenian warships gobbled all their figs.

TRYGAIOS.
And quite right too. *Their* warships gobbled *mine*.

CHORUS.
630   They wrecked my barn – they asked for all they got.

HERMES.
The people from the countryside came streaming in
To Athens. They didn't know, but they'd been sold
    as well.
They'd lost their crops, wanted compensation, *now*.
They looked at their leaders; their leaders looked
    at them,
Powerless, bankrupt, starving. The next step was
    obvious:
They shouted and yelled at Peace, and drove her out.
She kept coming back, of her own accord – she
    liked
The area – and every time, they threw her out
    again.
If anyone was fat and rich, they were crumbled

Like cake, for being in Spartan pay. And what
  about *you*?   640
Each time, like yapping dogs, you licked the crumbs.
You were pale with fear; they tossed you lies and scraps
Of slander; you gulped them down and howled for more.
The allies saw what was happening, and tried to stuff
The politicians' mouths with gold. So *they* grew rich,
Right under your noses, and Greece began to bleed
To death. Who was to blame? I shall now name names.
That tanner, for a start –

TRYGAIOS.

No, Hermes, no!
He's dead now, finished, not our concern but yours.   650
Call him what names you choose:
Blusterer, bastard, pisspot, skunk,
Con-artist, liar, pimple, drunk –
You're his patron god; you own the sod.

(*to* PEACE)

That's right, lady, isn't it? Why don't you speak?

HERMES.

She won't speak *here*. She's seen the audience.

TRYGAIOS.

She'll say a word or two to you.   660

HERMES.

Whisper, sweetheart. What d'you think about them
  now?
Sweet shield-and-buckler-hater, speak to me.

He listens.

Something's coming through. Yes. Yes. Yes. Right.
I'll tell you what she says the matter is.
It's you Athenians again. She says
She made a spontaneous initiative
Just after Pylos; she came to the Assembly
With a trayful of treaties, and still you threw her out.

TRYGAIOS.
    Sorry. Our minds were set on tanning hides.

HERMES *listens again*.

HERMES.
670   Mm. Right. She wants some information now.
    Who supports her? Who's her greatest enemy?

TRYGAIOS (*pointing into the audience*).
    Her biggest fan, by miles, is...Kleonymos.

HERMES.
    Him? Why?

TRYGAIOS (*into the audience*).
    Excuse me, sir, I think I heard
    A whisper of war.

HERMES.
    He's gone. He's run away.

TRYGAIOS.
    Exactly. *Her* best friend.

HERMES *listens*.

HERMES.
    She says, who's in charge
680   In Athens nowadays?

TRYGAIOS.
    Hyperbolos.
    Good heavens, what's the matter?

HERMES.
    You should hear
    What she thinks of that.
    Hyperbolos! What made you
    Trust a candle-maker?
    An oaf like that?

TRYGAIOS.
    We needed some light relief.   690

HERMES.
  She's off again. More questions.

TRYGAIOS.
  What?

HERMES.
  She's asking about her friends,
  From the good old days. How's Sophocles?

TRYGAIOS.
  He's never been the same
  Since *Oedipus*. Now he's such a Mummy's boy.[22]

HERMES.
  And how's that drunk Kratinos?

TRYGAIOS.
  Dead. He dropped   700
  A bottle, and died of a broken heart.
  Lady, things have been going from bad to worse.
  But now you're back, we'll not let go.

HERMES.
  In that case, I'll tell you exactly what to do.
  Take Harvest home, and marry her.
  Take her to the fields, plant sturdy vines.

TRYGAIOS.
  Come here, sweetheart. Give me a kiss.

  He kisses her, then takes HERMES *aside.*

  Er, look,
  Will it do any harm if I...I mean, if I...?   710
  You know how long it's been...

HERMES.
  Take some iron pills. You'll be all right.
  Don't forget this one. Holiday. Deliver her
  To the Assembly. They've had her there before.

TRYGAIOS.
  O lucky Assembly, to have your Holiday!

What a party you'll have! What steaks! What tripe!
Hermes, goodbye. Goodbye and thanks.

HERMES.
Goodbye,
Dear mortal. Off you go. Forget me not.

TRYGAIOS.
720   Pegasos! Pegasos! It's time to fly.

HERMES.
Ah. You won't see him again.

TRYGAIOS.
Why not?

HERMES.
He's been promoted. To Zeus' thunder-cart.

TRYGAIOS.
But what will the poor thing *eat*?

HERMES.
Ambrosia,
What else? Prepared in person by Ganymede.

TRYGAIOS.
And how will I get home?

HERMES.
Easy.
Right, past the goddess, and round the back.

TRYGAIOS.
Come on, girls, this way. Be quick. There are men
out there
Who've been working themselves up for you for
weeks.

He goes out with HARVEST *and* HOLIDAY[23].
HERMES *goes inside and closes Heaven's door.*

CHORUS.
On your way, then. Safe journey.
Now, coil those ropes.

The attendants will see to them.
Don't leave them *there!*
In the wings? Are you crazy?   730
They nick anything here
If it's not tied down. Good.
Ladies and gentlemen, interlude time[24].

Dance. Then:

When a writer of comedies starts
To recite his own praises, it's time
To make trouble and throw the man out.
But if any exception's allowed,
Then it's *him:* Aristophanes, prince
Of comedians, your author tonight.
All the others are formula men
With bad jokes about ragbags and lice,   740
Bakers, beggars and runaway slaves
Who've been beaten. (Not heard it before?
There's this slave, and he's crying, and his friend
Says, 'I told you. You can't knock the Boss
But the Boss can knock you.') What a load
Of old rubbish! He swept the stage clean
Of such garbage, and built up a style
Packed with towering arguments, jokes
With some point to them, poems and puns.   750
Not for *him* easy targets like X
Or like Y: he went straight to the top.
He was braver than Herakles, swam
Through the stink and the leather-lunged threats
Of the tannery, bearded the Beast
In its lair, with its eyes popping fire
And its tangle of toadies, its voice
Like a torrent of acid, its arse
Like a camel's, its seal-stink, its balls –
Oh those unwashed, incredible balls!
He was fearless. He grappled and fought
For the city of Athens, for *you.*   760
All he asks in return is – first prize.
If he wins, don't expect him to hang

About afterwards, looking for boys.
He'll just pack up his props and go home.
That's his recipe: laughter and tears
And, above all, impeccable taste.

(*in the original, in one breath*)

So we want you to clap
For him, gentlemen, boys.
Any bald-headed men
In the theatre tonight?
Clap as hard as you can.
If he wins, in the bar
770   And at dinner, they'll say,
'Good old Baldy! Drink up!
Bring Baldy the best!
He's the ace! In the race
For the comedy crown
He's a gleaming head-start!'

Muse, reject warfare, and sing
For our poet alone; come, and bring
Us enjoyment, sweet laughter and song,
780   Wine, dancing and pleasure all festival long.
But if Karkinos asks you
To join him, dear Muse,
That's one of the tasks you
Must simply refuse –
For he's past it, old-fashioned and bad.
What plays has this genius danced in?
All those where some dumb backer chanced him.
The Dwarves, The Quails, The Long-necked Cranes,
790   *It Never Pours Here, But It Rains* –
One number was nice,
In a play called *The Mice* –
But a cat ate it up in rehearsal. How sad!

All experienced poets soon learn
That as soon as the swallows return
800   To the woods and the whole world rejoices,
It's time with the Muses to lift up our voices.

But if Morsimos begs you
For help, dearest Muse,
His plays are just dregs you
Must simply refuse
To put in for a contest or crown.
With his brother to help him, he wrote
The following dramas of note:
The Greedy Pigs, The Harpies, Filthy Swine,   810
The Plague of Fish, Why Old Maids Whine –
Spit on poets like these;
Take Aristophanes
And dance for the festival, dance through the town!

Dance. When it ends, enter TRYGAIOS *from
the side-entrance beside his farm.*

TRYGAIOS.
  It's quite a walk, all the way from Heaven.
  My feet...!   820

  (*to the audience*)

  You've no idea how small you looked up there.
  Down here, of course, you're even worse.

A SLAVE *comes out of the farm.*

SLAVE.
  Hey, sir, you're back.

TRYGAIOS.
  I think so. Yes.

SLAVE.
  Good trip?

TRYGAIOS.
  Wearing. I wore my legs out, for a start.

SLAVE.
  Were you the only mortal man up there?

TRYGAIOS.
  Depends what you mean by *man.*
  There were one or two lyric poets...

SLAVE.

830 What doing?

TRYGAIOS.
 Harvesting odes. They float up there
 Like puffballs on a summer's day. *You* know.

SLAVE.
 So it's not true that when we die they make us
  stars?

TRYGAIOS.
 It's true.

SLAVE.
 Well, who's the latest star up there?

TRYGAIOS.
 Ion of Chios.

SLAVE.
 That puffball?

TRYGAIOS.
 There you are.

SLAVE.
 And what are all the comets and shooting stars?

TRYGAIOS.
840 After dinner, the rich stars go for a stroll,
 With fires in little pots to light the way.
 Now then...

 He goes to the side-entrance, and brings in
 HOLIDAY *and* HARVEST.

 Take this one inside. Warm some water
 And fill the tub. Make up a marriage-bed
 For her and me. Then come back here. I'll take
 The other one and hand her over.

SLAVE.
 Wow!
 Where did you pick *them* up?

TRYGAIOS.
In Heaven. Where else?

SLAVE.
You mean the gods go in for *that*? Just like us?
I'll not give tuppence for them now.

TRYGAIOS.
It can get very lonely, being a god.   850

SLAVE (*to* HARVEST).
Come over here, darling.
Hey, master, shall I give her something to eat?

TRYGAIOS.
Good heavens, no. She wouldn't know what to do
With mortal food. She's spent her time up there
Lapping ambrosia like all the other gods.

SLAVE.
We'll see to her lapping down here as well.

He takes HARVEST *inside.*

CHORUS.
What a lucky so-and-so!
Sails spread, course set for happiness.

TRYGAIOS.
Just wait till you see my wedding-suit.

CHORUS.
You'll be the flower of manhood,   860
Spreading your petals in sunny spring.

TRYGAIOS.
Just wait till I caress those breasts.

CHORUS.
You'll dance such pirouettes, such leaps!

TRYGAIOS.
Well, fair enough. Who flew?
Who beetled up to Heaven? Who
Saved everyone in Greece,

Brought luck,
A chance to fuck
And feast in peace?

Dance. When it ends, the SLAVE *comes out.*

SLAVE.
She's had her bath. You should see her glow!
We baked her buns and iced her cake.
870   The hen's on the nest; now all we need is – cock.

TRYGAIOS.
I'm coming. I just want to give this one
To the people. Holiday.

SLAVE.
Did you say Holiday?

TRYGAIOS.
What of it?

SLAVE.
I had her once. We all had her once.
We began with a drink –

TRYGAIOS (*to the audience*).
Ladies and gentlemen,
Can any of you be trusted? Any volunteers
To make sure she's handled right?
For the public good?

(*to the* SLAVE)

What are *you* doing?

SLAVE.
880   Practising.

TRYGAIOS (*to the audience*).
No takers?
Shall I pass her at random along the rows?

SLAVE.
Someone's waving over there.

TRYGAIOS.
Who?

SLAVE.
Ariphrades.
He says he'll have a go.

TRYGAIOS.
He says he'll have a *blow*,
You mean. Disgusting swine!

(*to* HOLIDAY)

Come over here, dear. That's right.
Put your things down. There we are.
Ladies and gentlemen[25], this is Holiday.
Consider all she has to offer.
Ah! I see several citizens
Rising already to welcome her.   890
Let me draw special attention to her barbecue.

SLAVE.
It's a little sooty. It saw a lot of use
Before the war – as you gentlemen well know.

TRYGAIOS.
As soon as she's yours you can hold your own
Olympic Games. Opening Ceremony – up and
    running.
Today's events: catch-as-catch-can, the crab,
The sideways wriggle, the shake, the poke.
Tomorrow: racing. The four-in-hand, the push –   900
They're panting, galloping, blowing hard
As they turn the last corner and take the fence...
Can they keep it up? Will we see them limp?
They're galloping, galloping, galloping –
Oh please, ladies and gentlemen,
Take Holiday. She's yours.

He hands her over to a CITIZEN *from the audience.*

SLAVE.
Did you see that? He can move when he wants to.

TRYGAIOS.
Well, wouldn't you? If *you* were him?
910   If *you'd* been holding your own for years?

CHORUS.
What an upright citizen!
Trygaios! What a man!

TRYGAIOS.
Just wait till harvest time. You'll see.

CHORUS.
Our benefactor,
Saviour, joy of the human race.

TRYGAIOS.
Just wait till you taste my next year's wine.

CHORUS.
You're our hero now, in the here-and-now.

TRYGAIOS.
Well, fair enough. Who braved
The powers on high? Who saved
920   Your bacon? Who huffed and puffed
For Greece?
Who said, 'If you can't make peace,
Get stuffed'?

Dance.

SLAVE.
What next?

TRYGAIOS.
We sacrifice to Peace.

SLAVE.
What with?

TRYGAIOS.
A leek?

SLAVE.
She doesn't need a leek.

TRYGAIOS.
  A fatted calf?

SLAVE.
  We ate the fatted calf.

TRYGAIOS.
  A sucking pig?

SLAVE.
  No luck. No suck.

TRYGAIOS.
  Well, what[26]?

SLAVE.
  A baa-lamb.   930

TRYGAIOS.
  Eh?

SLAVE.
  A baa-lamb.

TRYGAIOS.
  Oh, a *baa*-lamb! You fetch it.
  I'll set up the altar, here.

  He and the SLAVE *go in.*

CHORUS.
  When luck and the gods go hand in hand,
  Mortals reap the benefit. In the game of life   940
  They carry off first prize –

TRYGAIOS (*lugging out an altar*).
  And carry *on* an altar. *There!*

  He goes in again.

CHORUS.
  Snatch happiness, don't hesitate!
  The wintry wind of war
  Has changed. The hand of fate
  Gives luck for evermore.

*TRYGAIOS returns with equipment for the
sacrifice.*

TRYGAIOS.
Basket, barley-seeds, garland, carving-knife,
Firepot. What's holding up the lamb?

He shouts inside.

950   Oi! Can't you move faster?
There's a high risk
Of Chairis
The musical disaster.
He'll play for a slice
Of sacrifice,
He'll ask for charity,
Insist on parity.

The SLAVE *brings on a* SHEEP.

TRYGAIOS.
Right. Take the basket and the holy water
And walk round the altar. Left to right, for luck.

SLAVE.
There. What next?

TRYGAIOS.
I stick *this* in *here*...

He sprinkles the SHEEP *with water.*

960   Don't just stand there. Shake your head.

(to the SLAVE)

Give me some seeds.

He sprinkles the SHEEP *with barley.*

Give me the waterpot. Now, wash your hands
And sprinkle the audience with seeds.

SLAVE.
There.

TRYGAIOS.
That was quick.

SLAVE.
Quick, but thorough. There's not a man
In all that audience without a seed.

TRYGAIOS.
What about the women?

SLAVE.
They'll get theirs tonight.

TRYGAIOS.
Right then, let us pray.
Just a minute. We need a congregation.

SLAVE.
Here.

TRYGAIOS.
These sinners? You're joking.

SLAVE.
They're not sinners. Look: 970
They're moving their lips.
They're praying.

TRYGAIOS.
Let's start, then. Ready?

CHORUS.
Ready.

TRYGAIOS.
O lady of dancing and marriages, Peace,
Queen and goddess, accept our sacrifice.

SLAVE.
Yeah, lady, accept it. Don't play
Hide-and-seek with us,
Peep round the door at us,   980
Giggle and flirt with us,
Then disappear.

TRYGAIOS.
Come out like a lady, and show us your charms.
We've been dying to kiss you and take you in our
  arms
990 For ten long years.
Banish warfare,
Live up to your name,
And instead of the rumble and fuss
Of diplomacy, fill us with smiles
Of good fellowship,
Friendliness, trust.
Fill our markets with luxuries:
Cucumber, apples,
1000 Fresh figs,
Cloves of garlic, tarts,
Ducks, pigeons,
Quails, partridges,
Eels – oh, those succulent eels!
In the bustle and throng
Let that fool Melanthios arrive
Far too late;
1010 Let the goodies be gone.
Then, while everyone laughs
He can sing his own terrible songs:
Disaster! Disaster! I'll never find another!
They're gone! And never called me mother!
Grant these prayers,
Lady Peace, we pray.

SLAVE.
Right. Here's the knife. You sacrifice the lamb.
Go on, get stuck in.

TRYGAIOS.
I can't.

SLAVE.
Why not?

TRYGAIOS (*gesturing at the statue*).
1020 *She* wouldn't like it. Not out here.

Blood on the altar? Take it inside,
Do it there, and bring the bits out here.

(aside, as the SLAVE *removes the* SHEEP)*

We need it tomorrow, don't you know.
Another day, another show.

He starts making a fire on the altar.

CHORUS.
You're good at this.
A scatter of shavings, a twist of twigs,
Religiously arranged –

TRYGAIOS.
I'd make a perfect priest.

CHORUS.
Just right. For ability
And brains you set the pace;
For mental agility   1030
You win the race.

TRYGAIOS.
A match, a poke, a puff: it's holy smoke!
Now I'll fetch the table, and stir that slave.

He goes inside.

CHORUS.
You've got to admire him.
Quite unrattled
He battled
For Athens; nothing could tire him
Or turn him aside.
I glow with pride
To think of his clever
Endeavour.

TRYGAIOS *and the* SLAVE *come back.* TRYGAIOS *is
carrying a table; the* SLAVE *carries a leg of lamb.*

TRYGAIOS.
That's that, then. Put that down over here.
1040   I'll fetch the offal-plate and incense-pot.

SLAVE.
No, no. Let me.

He goes out.

TRYGAIOS.
Get on with it.

The SLAVE *returns with offal on a plate, and a pot
of smoking incense.*

SLAVE.
I'm back. What took me so long? Don't ask.

TRYGAIOS.
Start roasting these.

They begin to cook.

Don't look now,
But someone's coming with a laurel wreath.
Who is it?

SLAVE.
Some beggar. Some oracle-seller.

TRYGAIOS.
You're right. It's Hierokles.

SLAVE.
Oh god. What will *he* want?

TRYGAIOS.
He won't want peace.

SLAVE.
1050   He'll want a sniff of *this*.

TRYGAIOS.
Pretend you haven't seen him.

SLAVE.
Right.

Enter HIEROKLES.

HIEROKLES (*clearing his throat*).
Ha hoom. Of whom is this sacrifice in aid?

TRYGAIOS.
Don't put your hand in there.

HIEROKLES.
To whom is this sacrifice?

TRYGAIOS.
How's the parson's nose?

SLAVE.
Runny.

HIEROKLES.
Carve when ready.
Hand me the official slice.

TRYGAIOS.
It isn't cooked.

HIEROKLES.
That bit looks ready.

TRYGAIOS.
Don't handle the merchandise.

(*to the* SLAVE)

Time to carve. Where's the table? Bring the wine.

HIEROKLES.
The tongue's sliced separately, you know.

TRYGAIOS.
We know.   1060
D'you want to do something?

HIEROKLES.
Anything. What?

TRYGAIOS.
Shut up. While we sacrifice to Peace –

HIEROKLES.
  O YE MORTALS OF LITTLE BRAIN –

TRYGAIOS.
  It's story time.

HIEROKLES.
  DIM-WITTED AND GORMLESS, YE TURN
    FROM GOD
  AND WITH GIBBERING MONKEYS WALK
    HAND IN HAND –
  What's so funny?

TRYGAIOS.
  Gibbering monkeys? Look who's talking.

HIEROKLES.
  TENDER PIGEONS, YE NEST NOW WITH
    FERRETS.
  BEWARE THE FOXY GRIN, THE BEADY EYE –

TRYGAIOS.
  Beware hot air.
  Can't you use that scroll to fan the flames?

HIEROKLES.
  NAY! 'TIS WRITTEN. TO BAKIS THE NYMPHS
1070   FIRST WROTE;
  LORD BAKIS THEN WROTE WHAT THE
  NYMPHS FIRST WROTE
  TO LORD BAKIS –

TRYGAIOS.
  Take Bakis and stuff yourself!

HIEROKLES.
  'TIS NOT WRITTEN THAT PEACE IS TO LOSE
    HER CHAINS.
  FIRST OF ALL –

TRYGAIOS (to the SLAVE).
  First sprinkle some salt on.

HIEROKLES.
    'TIS NOT MEET UNTO HEAVEN TO MAKE PEACE
      YET.
    TILL THE WOLF LIETH DOWN WITH THE
      TENDER LAMB.

TRYGAIOS.
    No wolf's lying down with *this* tender lamb. Get lost!

HIEROKLES.
    WHILE THE BEETLE STILL FARTETH FORTH
      ITS FOULNESS,
    WHILE THE YAPPETY-FINCH BRINGETH
      FORTH BLIND PUPS,
    'TIS UNLAWFUL FOR MORTALS TO BRING
      PEACE BACK.

TRYGAIOS.
    What does Bakis suggest that we do instead?   1080
    Go on fighting? Cast lots who must weep most tears?
    Make a treaty with Sparta and carve up Greece?

HIEROKLES.
    CRABS WILL ALWAYS WALK SIDEWAYS.
      You'll not change that.

TRYGAIOS.
    NO FREE DINNERS FOR SCROUNGERS. You'll
      not change that.
    Don't you get it? We've peace now. We don't need
      this.

HIEROKLES.
    EVERY HEDGEHOG IS BRISTLY. You'll not
      change that.

TRYGAIOS.
    THIS ORACLE'S CROOKED. You'll not change
      that.

HIEROKLES.
    You've got proper authority to roast this sheep?

TRYGAIOS.

But of course. My own oracle. Here we are.
It's by Homer. Who else? And it goes like this:
FROM THE FOG AND BLACK NIGHT OF
1090   THE FIGHT THEY CAME;
THEY MADE PEACE AND A FEAST ROUND
THE ALTAR FIRE;
CARVED THE JOINT, FILLED THEIR
GOBLETS, PROCLAIMED HER NAME;
AND THE PROPHET GOT NOTHING AT ALL,
SO THERE.

HIEROKLES.

Ha! That's nothing but rubbish. Lord *Bakis* says –

TRYGAIOS.

Just a minute. There's more. Here's what *Homer*
says:
DETESTED, SHUNNED, OUTLAWED, BEYOND
THE PALE,
LET THE BLOOD-SPATTERED WAR-LOVER
WEEP AND WAIL.

HIEROKLES.

LO! THE VULTURES ARE GATHERING –

TRYGAIOS (*to the* SLAVE).

1100   Watch that lamb –
That's the first thing he's said that rings true to
me.
Pour the offering; bring me the meat; let's start.

HIEROKLES.

If it's all right with you, I'll just help myself.

He tries to suit action to words. But TRYGAIOS *is
pouring an offering of wine on the ground.*

TRYGAIOS.

Offering! Offering!

HIEROKLES.

Come on, pass it over, my share of the meat.

TRYGAIOS.
'TIS NOT MEET UNTO HEAVEN. I'll tell you
    what:
We'll begin with a prayer, and then you – clear off.
Stay with us, bless us forever, Peace, we pray.

HIEROKLES.
Carve the tongue.

TRYGAIOS.
Stick it out, then.

HIEROKLES (*grabbing for the wineskin*).
Offering!

TRYGAIOS (*hitting him with it*).
Here's an offering for you.   1110

HIEROKLES.
Just the tiniest slice –

TRYGAIOS.
WHEN THE TENDER LAMB
LIETH DOWN WITH THE WOLF.

HIEROKLES.
I beseech you. *Please.*

TRYGAIOS.
EVERY HEDGEHOG IS BRISTLY. I think you
    said.
Ladies and gentlemen, come up and join the feast.

HIEROKLES.
What can *I* eat?

TRYGAIOS.
Why don't you eat your Bakis? Here.

HIEROKLES.
I'm not leaving without a scrap of meat.

TRYGAIOS.
Have the scraps, then. Here.
Now what does Bakis say?

HIEROKLES.
I've had enough of this.

TRYGAIOS.
1120　Good. That's all you'll get.

(*to the* SLAVE)

Hit him with a stick.

SLAVE (*rummaging in* HIEROKLES' *sack*).
Just a minute. What's this?

TRYGAIOS.
A sheepskin? Is that ours?
It's *you* that's scavenging round the back?
Clear off. Fly away home. Shoo! Shoo!

He chases HIEROKLES *out*.

CHORUS.
Happiness! Happiness!
No more helmet,
No more onions, no more cheese.
1130　I never cared for the battle-line.
I like to sit by the fire
Drinking deep with friends
While the logs we chopped in summer
Crackle and blaze;
Roast nuts and acorns,
And while the wife takes a bath
Find a slave-girl and snatch a kiss.

1140　How's this for happiness? The sowing's done,
It's raining outside, and a neighbour calls.
'Hey, Komarchides,
What shall we do today?
Come round for a drink.
Leave Zeus to watch the crops.
Come and try the wife's bean stew,
Roast peanuts, figs.
Call the slaves inside.
It's far too wet out there

For pruning vines and hoeing.'
'Fine! I'll bring
A pigeon and a brace of finches. Yes –
And there's yoghurt too,
And four fat hares,   1150
Unless the cat's run off
With them: I heard
The most suspicious thuds
And bumps last night.
We'll have three of them,
And save the fourth for Dad.
Ask Aischinades to bring
A myrtle-branch.
Make it a date. Let's celebrate.'

Happiness! Happiness!
On summer days
When cicadas chirp and whirr,   1160
I love to test
The early grapes
For ripeness;
I love to watch
For the early-swelling fig,
To pick and eat,
To murmur, 'Happy days',
To mix a drink
Sharp with fresh-crushed thyme,
To grow comfortably plump,   1170
Sleek as a berry, all summer long.

How's that for happiness? Who'd rather watch
A major-general go strutting by,
All crests and scarlet cloak?
(He swears it's red
For blood; I say
It's red from blushing when
He sees the enemy
And fills his pants.)
Winged by his crests,
He turns and runs,

This cock of the walk,
While I stand firm and fight.
Back home, our hero muddles the call-up list,
Rubs some names out,
1180 Puts others in. You're due
On manoeuvres tomorrow.
You've not been told.
It's too late to buy provisions.
You see your name
On the list, and panic.
What else can you do?
Oh, he *owes* us country folk.
One day he'll pay,
1190 That peacock freak, that chicken-livered sneak.

Dance. Then TRYGAIOS *comes out, dressed in
wedding-clothes and carrying a helmet.*

TRYGAIOS.
Eeoo, eeoo!
What a wedding-party! What a crowd of guests!

He passes the helmet to someone inside.

Here. Use the crest for sponging tables.
It's good for nothing else.
You can serve the thrushes now,
The rolls, the rabbit stew.

Enter SICKLE-MAKER.

SICKLE-MAKER.
Where's Trygaios?

TRYGAIOS.
Here. That's me.

SICKLE-MAKER.
My dear!
You've done us such a good turn, rescuing Peace.
1200 Before, in wartime, we couldn't shift our stock
For love or money. Now, it fetches its weight
In gold. Oh, thank you, thank you. Here you are:

A wedding-present. Here. And here. Oh, look,
Why not take the lot? Your share of the profit.
  There.

TRYGAIOS.
  Wheel them inside, and join the party. Thanks.
  Go on – there's someone else arriving now.

  The SICKLE-MAKER *goes inside. Enter*
  ARMOURER *and* FRIENDS.

ARMOURER.
  Trygaios, I'm ruined, thanks to you.

TRYGAIOS.
  What's wrong with you? Plume-onia?   1210

ARMOURER.
  My livelihood –
  It's taken a hammering. And look at him:
  He's reached rock-bottom. So has he...

TRYGAIOS.
  How much are you asking for crests like these?

ARMOURER.
  How much are you offering?

TRYGAIOS.
  This socket's neatly worked...three bags of figs.
  We're short of dusters.

ARMOURER.
  Fetch the figs: it's yours.

  (*to his* FRIENDS)

  It's better than nothing. Three bags! Of figs!   1220

TRYGAIOS.
  Just a minute. Get rid of it!
  It's moulting! Revolting thing!
  I'm not paying good figs for that!

ARMOURER.
  What about a breastplate? Really cheap.

TRYGAIOS.
Now you're talking.
We're dotty for potties.

ARMOURER.
Pardon?

TRYGAIOS.
Look:
I turn it this way up, I fetch some stones,
1230   I sit like this – hey presto.

ARMOURER.
Oh, brilliant! How d'you wipe your bum?

TRYGAIOS.
Through the armholes. Here and here.

ARMOURER.
Through both at once?

TRYGAIOS.
Why not, when you're having such good, clean fun?

ARMOURER.
You'd pay a thousand drachs
For a potty?

TRYGAIOS.
Of course.

He hitches up his clothes and squats.

ARMOURER.
Fetch the money, quick.

TRYGAIOS (*leaping up*).
No good. It chafes.
I'm not buying *that*.

ARMOURER.
1240   A bugle, perhaps?

TRYGAIOS.
Let's see.
If you poured some lead in *here*,

And stuck a stick up *here*,
You could use it for skittles.

ARMOURER.
Ha, ha.

TRYGAIOS.
No, I'm serious.
Tie a string to this end,
Add a pole, you've got a pair of fig-scales.

ARMOURER.
And what about *him*? Those crests?   1250
He paid a drachma a dozen for plumes like those.

TRYGAIOS.
Tell him to go to Egypt. Fly-whisks.
They're crazy for fly-whisks there.

ARMOURER.
Aaee! Fellow-armourers, we've had it here.

TRYGAIOS.
No, *he's* all right.

ARMOURER.
Who'll buy his helmets now?

TRYGAIOS.
Everyone, if he sticks handles on the sides
And calls them jugs.

ARMOURER (*to his* FRIENDS).
Let's go.   1260

TRYGAIOS.
I want to buy some spears.

ARMOURER.
How much?

TRYGAIOS.
Sawn in half, they're ideal for vine-poles.
Two drachs the hundred.

ARMOURER.

> He's insulting us. Come on.

TRYGAIOS.

> Clear off, why don't you? There's someone coming
> out.

Exeunt ARMOURER *and* FRIENDS. *Two* BOYS
come out of the farm.

> Hello. Come out for wee-wees?
> Are your Daddies at the party?
> Are you going to recite for us afterwards?
> A party-piece? That's nice. Come over here,
> And try a line or two now. You start.

FIRST BOY.

1270   *O for a Muse of fire –*

TRYGAIOS.

> Hang on, hang on.
> You little bastard, who needs a Muse of fire
> In peace-time? Don't they teach you *anything*?

FIRST BOY.

> *Leashed in like hounds, should famine, sword and fire*
> *Crouch for employment –*

TRYGAIOS.

> Famine, sword, fire? I'm still not keen.
> Try something else.

FIRST BOY.

> What else? *You* choose.

TRYGAIOS.

1280   How about *Here comes the bride, Dumdee, dahdee wide –* ?

FIRST BOY.

> *A loaf of bread, a jug of wine, and thou –*

TRYGAIOS.

> I like that. You can't beat jugs of wine.

FIRST BOY.
The boy stood on the burning deck –

TRYGAIOS.
For god's sake, stop! Sea-battles, now!
Don't you know anything but war?
What's your Daddy's name?

FIRST BOY.
What? Mine?

TRYGAIOS.
Yes. Yours.

FIRST BOY.
General Lamachos.   1290

TRYGAIOS.
I knew it. General Lamachos,
General nuisance. Out!

He shoos him out, then turns to the other BOY.

What's *your* Daddy's name?

SECOND BOY.
Kleonymos.

TRYGAIOS.
That's more like it.
Old Blubberguts' son won't talk of war.

SECOND BOY.
Last night I danced with fairies in the wood –

TRYGAIOS.
Whose little boy did you say you were?   1300

SECOND BOY.
I shucked my shield –

TRYGAIOS.
Oh, come inside.

(*to the* CHORUS)

It's party time. Don't lag behind.
Unleash your choppers. Grind
And gormandise and chew.
Crunch! Munch! It's up to you
With man-size, pan-size bites
1310   To exercise your pearly-whites.

He and the SECOND BOY *go inside*.

CHORUS.
Superbly put. Oh, very nice.
Friends, follow his advice.
Pick up your bellies, grab
A plate of rabbit, nab
Some cake. Make your requests –
The party's started, and you're the guests.

Music.

Make way! Make way! Fetch the lovely bride,
Lift high your torches, dance and sing.
Home to the fields, lead on, lead on!
Pour offerings, jump for joy and shout.
Yay, Peace! Hyperbolos, get out!
1320   Pray Heaven to bless us all,
To shower Greece
With wealth, wine, golden crops,
Figs, feasts, fertility,
Happy, golden days,
Everlasting peace –
Let war forever cease.

Enter TRYGAIOS *and* HARVEST *in procession,
as bride and groom*.

TRYGAIOS.
Come, beloved, to the fields.
Lie there with me,   1330
Bless me with bliss.

CHORUS.
   Hymen, Hymenaios, O!
   Hymen, Hymenaios, O!

   O happy man, O blest,
   O rightly blest,
   Reap your reward.
   Hymen, Hymenaios, O!
   Hymen, Hymenaios, O!

   Lift up the bride,
   Lift up the groom.
   Hymen, Hymenaios, O!   1340

   Be lucky! Live lives
   Of peace and joy.
   Hymen, Hymenaios, O!

TRYGAIOS.
   What shall I do with her?

CHORUS A.
What shall he do with her?

CHORUS B.
   Harvest her, harvest her.

CHORUS.
   Harvest her, harvest her.

CHORUS A.
   His is long and thick.

CHORUS.
   Hymen, Hymenaios, O!

CHORUS B.
   Hers is plump and ripe.   1350

CHORUS.
   Hymen, Hymenaios, O!

TRYGAIOS.
   On, to the feast –

CHORUS.
Hymen, Hymenaios, O!

TRYGAIOS.
On, to the wedding-feast.

CHORUS.
Hymen, Hymenaios, O!

The procession begins to move off.

CHORUS (*to the audience*).
Ladies and gentlemen, happiness!
Join in. There's cake for one and all.
Hymen, Hymenaios O!
Hymen, Hymenaios O!

Exeunt omnes in procession.

LYSISTRATA

Characters

LYSISTRATA
KALONIKE
MYRRHINE
LAMPITO
THEBAN WOMAN
COMMISSIONER
DEFECTOR
OLD MAN
OLD WOMAN
KINESIAS
BABY
SPARTAN MESSENGER
DOORKEEPER (female)
SPARTAN AMBASSADOR
ATHENIAN CITIZEN

silent parts:

ATHENIAN MEN
ATHENIAN WOMEN
CONSTABLES
CORINTHIAN WOMAN
ORDERLY
RECONCILIATION
SERGEANT
SLAVE
SPARTAN MEN

CHORUS OF OLD MEN (CHORUS A)
CHORUS OF OLD WOMEN (CHORUS B)

*Open space. Centre back, the Propylaia, the imposing
gateway to the Acropolis. To one side, Pan's Grotto.
Dawn.* LYSISTRATA *is waiting.*

LYSISTRATA.

    This is ridiculous! If they'd been asked to come
    To some festival – for Bacchos or Aphrodite, say –
    We wouldn't be able to *move* for castanets.
    But as it is: deserted. Not a woman in sight.
    Except...who's that, next door? Kalonike?

    Enter KALONIKE.

KALONIKE.

    Good heavens, Lysistrata,
    What's the matter? What *are* you scowling at?
    Your eyebrows look as though they're taking off.

LYSISTRATA.

    Kalonike, it's women. They're getting me down.
    I'm furious. Our husbands are quite right: 10
    We *are* only good for one thing.

KALONIKE.

    But we *are* good at that.

LYSISTRATA.

    I sent out invitations. Every woman in Greece.
    SOMETHING REALLY IMPORTANT. COME AT
       ONCE.
    And where are they? Tucked up in bed, asleep.

KALONIKE.

    They'll be here. You know how hard it is
    For women to get out in the morning.
    Wake up the slaves, see to His Nibs,
    Bath the baby, feed it, burp it –

LYSISTRATA.

    Burping babies! There's more to life than that!   20

KALONIKE.

    Lysistrata, dear, what *is* it?
    Why have you called us? Is it important?

LYSISTRATA.
Something's come up.

KALONIKE.
Ah. Big?

LYSISTRATA.
Far-reaching.

KALONIKE.
And they're still not here?

LYSISTRATA.
It's sensitive.
I've been turning it over, night after night,
For weeks.

KALONIKE.
No wonder it's sensitive.

LYSISTRATA.
Tell me, Kalonike:
If all we women in Greece got together,
30   D'you think we could save the country?

KALONIKE.
You're joking.

LYSISTRATA.
Of course I'm not joking. This is war.
How's it to end? Is Sparta to be smashed?

KALONIKE.
Sounds good to me.

LYSISTRATA.
Is Thebes to be thrashed?

KALONIKE.
Oh yes – if they spare those lovely Theban eels.

LYSISTRATA.
Is Athens to be – there isn't a word that fits.
But if every woman in Greece turned up here
    today,

From Sparta, from Thebes, from here, from
    everywhere,   40
Don't you think we could end the war forever?

KALONIKE.
How can *women* end the war? Silk dresses,
Flowers in the hair, fancy slippers,
That *dreamy* new scent – that's all we know.

LYSISTRATA.
That's all we need. Flower-garlands,
Fancy slippers, dresses in see-through silk...

KALONIKE.
I don't understand.

LYSISTRATA.
When I've finished,
No man will ever raise a spear again.   50

KALONIKE.
I could wear that *daffodil* silk...

LYSISTRATA.
Or swing a sword.

KALONIKE.
That gorgeous negligée...

LYSISTRATA.
Or wield a shield.

KALONIKE.
I *must* buy some shoes.

LYSISTRATA.
That's what I want them here for.

KALONIKE.
If they'd known, they'd have *flown*.

LYSISTRATA.
I'm not surprised the Athenians are late.
They always are. But our friends from Salamis –

KALONIKE.
Fishermen's wives. You're right. That's odd.
60   They're usually up so early. To catch the tide.

LYSISTRATA.
I really expected the Acharnians...

KALONIKE.
I did see Theagenes' wife just now.
'Tally ho. We're hoisting sail. We're on our way.'

LYSISTRATA.
Aha. Here's someone now.

KALONIKE.
Oh yes.

LYSISTRATA.
Someone else...someone else...

KALONIKE.
Puah! Where on Earth are *they* from?

LYSISTRATA.
The Swamps.

KALONIKE.
I think they brought them with them.

Enter WOMEN, *including* MYRRHINE.

MYRRHINE.
Are we too late, Lysistrata? We came
As fast as we could. You *do* look cross.

LYSISTRATA.
70   You're *late*, Myrrhine. I said it was important.

MYRRHINE.
Yes, well, you see, I was groping in the dark
For *ages*. I couldn't find my belt.
Anyway, what is it? We're here now.

LYSISTRATA.
We'll wait till everyone arrives.
They're coming all the way from Sparta...Thebes...

Dirty

MYRRHINE.
Yes, so they are. Look: Lampito.

Enter more WOMEN, *led by* LAMPITO.

LYSISTRATA.
Lampito, darling, how are things in Sparta?
My goodness, you do look pretty...um...fit.   80
You look as if you could break a bull.

LAMPITO[27].
I did, this morning.
It's my exercise plan. You crouch, like this,
You make a controlled spring, and kick your own bum.

LYSISTRATA.
Good for the figure. Ladies, look.

LAMPITO.
No touching, please.

LYSISTRATA.
And who's this young beauty here?

LAMPITO.
The delegate from Thebes.

LYSISTRATA.   chested
She certainly is delicate. What a fine, flat plain.

LAMPITO.
Freshly plucked and mown.

LYSISTRATA.
And who's this here?

LAMPITO.
The lassie from Corinth.   90

LYSISTRATA.   arse
I should have known by the canal.

LAMPITO.
Well now, who was it who called us here?

LYSISTRATA.
It was me.

LAMPITO.
What for?

MYRRHINE.
Ooh, yes, Lysistrata, tell us everything.

LYSISTRATA.
In a minute. You tell *me* something first.

MYRRHINE.
Anything at all. Just ask.

LYSISTRATA.
Just think of your husbands for a moment...
100   The fathers of your children. Up at the front,
Every one of them. Don't you miss them?

KALONIKE.
Mine's been away in Thrace for months.
Five months! Keeping an eye on that general...
Whatsisname.

MYRRHINE.
Mine's been in Pylos for...ooh, ages.

LAMPITO.
Mine falls out, comes home, re-equips, and runs.

LYSISTRATA.
You see what I mean. No husbands, no lovers
To blow on the embers.

MYRRHINE.
No embers.

KALONIKE.
If Miletos hadn't defected, there might still have
been
110   Eight inches of leather between us and...

LYSISTRATA.
Tell me, ladies, if I found a way to end the war,
Would you do *anything* to help?

MYRRHINE.
Oh yes. I'd even pawn this dress,
If it would pay for a toast to Peace.

KALONIKE.
Me too. For Peace, they could fillet me
Like a turbot, and sell the biggest half.

LAMPITO.
If Peace was at the top, I'd climb Taÿgetos.
Mountain-range. Where weaklings are exposed.

LYSISTRATA.
All right, ladies. It's time to tell my plan.
If we really want our men to end this war,   120
All we have to do is give up...

MYRRHINE.
What?

LYSISTRATA.
I can't. It's too much to ask.

MYRRHINE.
Of course you can. Give up what? Our lives?

LYSISTRATA.
No. Sex. What's the matter?
Where are you going? Don't turn away.
You're frowning. You're pale. You're crying.
Will you or won't you? It's now or never.

MYRRHINE.
Lysistrata, I *can't*. Let the war drag on.

KALONIKE.
Out of the question, dear. Let the war drag on.   130

LYSISTRATA.
What? My own little turbot? A moment ago
You were going to be filleted and sold.

KALONIKE.
>I don't mind fillets. I'd walk through fire.
>But not...not *that*. Anything else.
>Not *that*, dear. No.

LYSISTRATA.
>What about you?

THEBAN.
>What she said. Fire.

LYSISTRATA.
>*Frailty, thy name is woman.* As someone said.
>We just won't kick against the pricks.
140 We just won't kick against the pricks.
>Lampito, darling Lampito, it's up to you.
>If Sparta agrees, if only Sparta's with me,
>We may still do it.

LAMPITO.
>It's a hard thing to ask.
>We don't go to bed to sleep, in Sparta.
>Kick against the pricks, you say? Ah well,
>If it's the only way. Let Peace come first.

LYSISTRATA.
>Oh, you darling! The only real woman here.

KALONIKE.
>But even if we *did* give up...give up...
>And Heaven forbid we should...how would it *work*?

LYSISTRATA.
>Simple. We sit there...
>Wearing nothing but a dab of perfume...
150 Or perhaps one of those nighties from Amorgos...
>We pluck and trim our entrances,
>Like good little spiders...the flies come strolling in...
>Caught! They're begging for it, hard –
>And what do we do? We just don't want to know.
>They'll be falling over themselves to give us peace.

LAMPITO.
Like Menelaus, whenever Helen bared a breast.
Sheathed his sword to the hilt, every single time.

KALONIKE.
But what if they *believe* us? Turn round, march out?

LYSISTRATA.
Then it's back to carrots, as the proverb says.

MYRRHINE.
I never could stand proverbs. Or carrots.
What if they...drag us into the bedroom...   160
Try to force us...

LYSISTRATA.
Hang on to the doorpost.

MYRRHINE.
What if they...smack our bottoms?

LYSISTRATA.
Turn the other cheek.
Smile sweetly. There are a thousand ways.
Don't give them the pleasure. They'll soon give up.

MYRRHINE.
If you really think we should...

LAMPITO.
You can rely on our Spartan chappies.
One, two, three. We'll bring 'em to heel.
But your Athenians. Flabby lot. Who'll see to them?   170

LYSISTRATA.
We'll stiffen them, don't worry.

LAMPITO.
But why should *they* want peace? They've ships,
And ropes, and war-funds here in the Acropolis.

LYSISTRATA.
That's all in hand. We're taking it over.
The Acropolis. Today. Complete with treasury.
There's a party of..ahem...older ladies on duty now.

While we strip for action *here*, they go up *there*.
They pretend they want to sacrifice – and *bam*!

LAMPITO.

180   *Bam*, eh? I like the sound of that. What next?

LYSISTRATA.

We swear an oath. A solemn, binding oath.

LAMPITO.

Ready when you are. You name, we'll swear.

LYSISTRATA.

Orderly!

Enter ORDERLY.

Stop gaping, woman. Put that shield down, here.
The other way up. Now fetch a leg of lamb.

KALONIKE.

A leg of lamb? What sort of oath is this?

LYSISTRATA.

A peace-oath. On a piece of meat.
Why a lamb? *Like a lamb to the slaughter...*
You remember.

KALONIKE.

It's peace, dear.
190   We can't use slaughtered lambs, or shields.

LYSISTRATA.

What else would you suggest?

MYRRHINE.

A white horse would be nice.
I always feel I could do anything at all,
On a white horse.

LYSISTRATA.

Have you got one handy?

MYRRHINE.

Ooh. No.

KALONIKE.
>   I know. We take a big, black bowl,
>   And a long-necked wineskin. We sacrifice...
>   We drink that lovely blood, and swear that oath.

LAMPITO.
>   That's the oath for me!

LYSISTRATA.
>   Orderly! Lose lamb. Bring bowl. Big, black.
>   And a skin of wine.

>   *The* ORDERLY *does as ordered.*

MYRRHINE.
>   Isn't he *lovely*?   200
>   I don't think I could refuse him *anything*.

LYSISTRATA.
>   Put it *down*. Now, everyone take hold.
>   Persuasion, hear our prayers;
>   Help feminine affairs,
>   Our grand design,
>   As we pour the wine.

KALONIKE.
>   What a gorgeous colour. Look how it *spurts*!

LAMPITO.
>   Gods, what a lovely smell!

MYRRHINE.
>   Me first. Let me swear first.

KALONIKE.
>   Please! There *is* a queue.

LYSISTRATA.
>   Stand in a circle and touch the bowl.
>   Say the words after me. Ready?   210
>   I swear I'll never let in my direction –

LAMPITO.
>   I swear I'll never let in my direction –

LYSISTRATA.
A gentleman in full erection –

M

KALONIKE.
A gentleman in full erection.
My legs have gone all wobbly.

LYSISTRATA.
I'll sit at home in sheerest silk –

MYRRHINE.
I'll sit at home in sheerest silk –

LYSISTRATA.
Sweet-scented, skin as white as milk –

LAMPITO.
220 Sweet-scented, skin as white as milk –

LYSISTRATA.
And if he tries to have me, I'll say no –

KALONIKE.
And if he tries to have me, I'll say no –

LYSISTRATA.
I'll kick and scream, I'll struggle so –

MYRRHINE.
I'll kick and scream, I'll struggle so –

LYSISTRATA.
No legs arched high to touch the ceiling –

LAMPITO.
230 No legs arched high to touch the ceiling –

LYSISTRATA.
No doggy-crouch, for extra feeling –

KALONIKE.
No doggy-crouch, for extra feeling –

LYSISTRATA.
And if I yield, and break this vow –

MYRRHINE.
  And if I yield, and break this vow –

LYSISTRATA.
  No wine for me, but water now –

LAMPITO.
  No wine for me, but water now.

LYSISTRATA.
  You all agree to this?

MYRRHINE.
  Yes, yes.

LYSISTRATA.
  Good. I'll consecrate the offering.

KALONIKE.
  Leave some for the rest of us.
  Remember: all for one and one for –

  Shouting, off.

LAMPITO.
  Castor and Pollux, what was that?

LYSISTRATA.
  It's all right: I told you.   240
  The old women have captured the Acropolis.
  Lampito, darling, off you go: start things up
  In Sparta. Leave *them* here as hostages.
  We'll go inside, bolt ourselves in, get organised.

KALONIKE.
  But what if the men attack straight away?

LYSISTRATA.
  Let them. They won't get past me.   250
  Threats, shouts, fire, no way. Except on our terms.
  If they want a piece, they must offer: peace.

KALONIKE.
  'Can't argue with a woman'. They keep saying that.
  So now they'll find it's true.

2/

Exeunt, LAMPITO *at the side, the others through
the centre doorway, which they close behind them.*

Music. Enter CHORUS OF OLD MEN (CHORUS A).
They are carrying branches; one has a firepot.

CHORUS A.
Come on, old fellow, hurry up.
Of course your shoulder's sore.
Of course it is, it's bound to be:
Look what you're carrying.

How could this happen, men?
Could anything be worse?
260   The wives we loved and cherished –
A pain, a plague, a curse.
Our own Acropolis,
The symbol of our state –
They've locked themselves inside it,
They've barred the sacred gate.

Don't just stand there. Pile the branches.
Green and sappy. Round the doorway.
Make a bonfire. Now they're for it.
Smoke 'em out. They'll soon come running.
270   Coughing, crying. They'll surrender.

D'you remember the last time we'd someone holed
    up here
In the Acropolis? That Spartan, Kleomenes?
Gods, what a siege that was!
We made that Spartan growl.
How proud he was! How boastful!
And how we made him howl!
He shouted, 'I surrender';
We stood here, rank by rank.
He slunk out, starving, whining;
280   He flapped his rags. He stank.

Now it's women. Barred and bolted.
Playing soldiers. What a business!
Who'd have thought it? Who'll endure it?

We won at Marathon, beat Persia –
They won't face us. They'll surrender.

Up here.
Don't flag, don't flinch.
We're near.
Another inch.
My shoulders are falling apart.
I wish I'd a donkey and cart.   290
A little higher.
Who's got the fire?
Look at it glow.
Are you ready? Blow.
Fff, fff, ee, oo,
It's smoking, groo!

It bites.
It's got fangs, got wings.
It fights.
It nips and stings.
It's choking me. This isn't funny.   300
My eyes are all red-rimmed and runny.
Athene, please!
We're on our knees.
Don't let it stay.
Blow it away.
Fff, fff, ee, oo,
It's still here. Groo!

That's well alight. Put the branches down.
What next? Light the torches?
Hammer on the door? A battering ram?
But what if they refuse to open up?
Do we set fire to the whole damn thing   310
And force 'em out that way? Dunno, dunno.
At least we've put that firewood down.
Give our shoulders a break, if you see what I mean.

(to the audience)

Any of you gentlemen like to lend a hand?
Any generals in the house?

Never mind. Light the torches. Me first.
Stick 'em in the firepot, burn up bright.
Lady Victory, help us punish that female pride.
We'll put up a trophy as soon as we get inside.

They begin lighting their torches at the firepot.
Enter CHORUS OF OLD WOMEN (CHORUS B),
carrying water.

CHORUS B.
    Smoke! Someone's playing with fire.
320   This way, ladies. Hurry. Here.

    Don't stand there! You'll stifle.
    A lungful, an eyeful.
    Those silly old jokers
    Are trying to smoke us.
    Bring water and put them out now.

    Here's a potful, a mugful,
    A bowlful, a jugful.
330   I managed to get some.
    Those grandads, we'll wet some,
    We'll soak them and put them out now.

    Such moaning and mumbling,
    Such groaning and grumbling!
    No bath-house, no pyre would
    Need half as much firewood.
    Bring water and put it out now.

340   Athene will hear us.
    She's bound to stand near us.
    The weather-god's daughter
    Knows all about water.
    She'll soak them and put them out now.

Dance; stand-off.

Stop that!
Don't *do* that.
You can't do that in a holy place.   350

CHORUS A.
    It's hardly holy now.
    It's swarming with females.

CHORUS B.
    You're shaking. You're trembling. Why?
    Because you're outnumbered? Because
    We've thousands more, inside?

CHORUS A.
    This boasting is silly. Who's got
    An olive branch? The symbol of peace?
    Wallop 'em with it. Let's *have* some peace.

CHORUS B.
    Put your pots in a circle, ladies.
    Roll up your sleeves.
    We're being attacked.

CHORUS A.
    A left and a right to the jaw.   360
    Like that boxer Boupalos.
    That'll shut their yap.

CHORUS B.
    Don't you touch my yap,
    If you want to keep your balls.

CHORUS A.
    Two lovely black eyes.

CHORUS B.
    You're joking.

CHORUS A.
    A cauliflower ear.

CHORUS B.
    You're senile.

CHORUS A.
You're for it.

CHORUS B.
You're past it.

CHORUS A.
You've had it.

CHORUS B.
Just try me.

CHORUS A.
Euripides!

CHORUS B.
Pardon?

CHORUS A.
That sex is damned, by Heaven cursed:
The female sex, of every sex the worst.

CHORUS B.
370   Right. Where's that water-jug?

CHORUS A.
Cursed of the gods, you dare bring water here?

CHORUS B.
Well, *you* brought fire. Go scorch yourself.

CHORUS A.
I'll burn you like a bonfire.

CHORUS B.
I'll soak you like seaweed.

CHORUS A.
Like seaweed?

CHORUS B.
Like seaweed.

CHORUS A.
A touch of torch?

CHORUS B.
  A bowl of bath?

CHORUS A.
  You and whose army?

CHORUS B.
  Make my day.

CHORUS A.
  Make *my* day.

CHORUS B.
  My day.   380

CHORUS A.
  Burn her hair off.

CHORUS B.
  Ladies...

  Shower of water.

CHORUS A.
  Yarg!

CHORUS B.
  What's the matter? Too cold for you?

CHORUS A.
  What are you *doing*?

CHORUS B.
  Watering your shoot, to see how it grows.

CHORUS A.
  It's withering. I'm shivering.

CHORUS B
  What a shame your fire's gone out.
  You could have warmed yourself on that.

  Enter COMMISSIONER *and* CONSTABLES.

COMMISSIONER.
  Has it blazed up again? The female sex:
  Its impertinence, its orgies, its castanets.

Howling and yowling, like pussies on a roof!
390 D'you remember yesterday? In full Assembly!
That fool Demostratos was making a motion,
Something about sailing for Sicily,
And all the while his wife kept prancing round
Shouting 'Weep! Weep for Adonis!'
'We'll send zealots from Zakynthos to cut 'em off',
He said. And *she* said (I think she'd had a few),
'Cut 'em. Cut 'em for Adonis!' *He* said...*she* said...
He said...*she* said...it went on all morning.
I don't know which of them was worse.

CHORUS A.
I'll tell you what's worse, sir. *Them.*
400 They've splashed us and soaked us and splattered us.
We're *dripping*. You'd think we'd pissed ourselves.

COMMISSIONER.
Poseidon, lord of water! That's no joke.
The whole thing's no joke. It's your own damn
        fault.
It's men in general who're to blame for this.
We're far too nice to them. We pamper them,
We spoil them. And it soon gets out of hand.
You go to the jeweller, the goldsmith. You say,
'Remember that necklace you made for my lady
        wife?
410 She was dancing last night and the pin fell out.
I've got to sail to Salamis tomorrow:
Run up to the house, there's a good fellow,
And put in a pin for her.' Or else –
You know that cobbler? Short little man,
Like a little boy, except for the – yes, *that* one.
'My wife's sandal is rubbing her little toe.
Slip up today, and ease the strain for her.'
420 That's how it starts – and look at the result.
Here am I, Commissioner for Shipping,
Come here to the City Treasury for cash
To buy oars for our gallant lads at sea –
And what do I find? Gates shut, doors barred,

And a bunch of women, squatting. It just won't do.
Constable, that crowbar. We'll put a stop to this.
Don't stand there gaping.
Stick your tool under there, and lift.
Oh here, let me.

LYSISTRATA *comes out.*

LYSISTRATA.
It's open: look. No trouble.   430
It isn't tools you need, it's common sense.

COMMISSIONER.
Common sense? A commissioner of state?
Constable! Arrest that woman.

LYSISTRATA.
Don't touch me! That is,
If you ever want to eat again.

COMMISSIONER.
Pay no attention. What are you afraid of?
Grab her round the middle.

CHORUS B.
Touch her, by god, and shit yourself.   440

COMMISSIONER.
He has already. Someone else. You, man.
Grab that one: the one making all the noise.

CHORUS B.
Lay one finger on her, and lose it.

COMMISSIONER.
I said *batter*, not *scatter*.
Block the exit.

CHORUS B.
I'll block theirs first.

COMMISSIONER.
Good grief, they've gone.
Come back. They're women: 450
Don't let them get on top. Come back.

LYSISTRATA.
> I'm warning you.
> There are four more companies inside.
> BIG ladies, armed to the TEETH and WILD.

COMMISSIONER.
> Don't just stand there. Grab!

LYSISTRATA.
> Women of Athens, help!
> WheatgermandpoppyseedwholemealandPITTAgirls,
> GarlicandonionandbeetrootandCARROTgirls,
> Grab, bite, gouge, pinch, tear, rip, scratch.

> WOMEN *appear from all sides. Melée.*

460   Don't be bashful! Don't be shy!

> *The* CONSTABLES *run for it.*

> That's it, now. Leave them. Heel, girls, heel!

COMMISSIONER.
> Them: four. Us: nil. Not a good result, for us.

LYSISTRATA.
> Well, what did you expect? What did you take us
>   for?
> Did you imagine women had no spirit, no bottle?

COMMISSIONER.
> No bottle? I'd rather not answer that.

CHORUS A.
> Quite right, sir. Don't waste your breath
> On them. They're maniacs, wild beasts.
> Just look at the bath they've given us –
470   Fully dressed, soapless – they're hopeless.

CHORUS B.
> I warned you: make my day, I said.
> And did you listen? With *that* thick ear?
> All I want is to sit quietly at home...like this.
> I want to be tidy and calm...like this.
> But someone always comes along and pulls my chain.

CHORUS A.
 They're fiends in human shape.
 But we can't just stand and gape.
 We have to try.
 We must ask why   480
 Such outrage, such disgrace
 In Athene's holy place.
 It won't be easy. Not a pleasant task.
 But it has to be done. Go on, sir: ask.

COMMISSIONER.
 Very well. It's simple, ladies. First,
 Why in Zeus' name have you barred these gates?

LYSISTRATA.
 To keep *you* out of the Treasury. No cash, no war.

COMMISSIONER.
 What's war to do with cash?

LYSISTRATA.
 You're joking!
 Public upset, hubble bubble, turmoil and trouble –
 Meat and drink to every politician ever born.
 (Remember Peisandros?) *Why*, did you say? Because
 When the state's in a mess, they get the job   490
 Of sorting things out – and *then* they're in clover,
 A snout in every trough. Well, things have changed.
 We've got the trough. We've got the cash.
 You can hubble and bubble all you like, it's ours.

COMMISSIONER.
 And what will you do with it?

LYSISTRATA.
 Look after it.

COMMISSIONER.
 Look after money? Women?

LYSISTRATA.
 What's wrong with that?
 We manage the housekeeping, don't we?

COMMISSIONER.
  That's different.

LYSISTRATA.
  How?

COMMISSIONER.
  Because *this* money's set aside for making war.

LYSISTRATA.
  We've abolished war.

COMMISSIONER.
  That's that, then. We're done for.

LYSISTRATA.
  Of course you aren't. We'll protect you.

COMMISSIONER.
  You?

LYSISTRATA.
  Us.

COMMISSIONER.
  Huh.

LYSISTRATA.
  You'll see.

COMMISSIONER.
  It's ridiculous.

LYSISTRATA.
  It's common sense.

COMMISSIONER.
500 It's out of the question.

LYSISTRATA.
  You'll still be saved.

COMMISSIONER.
  And if I won't?

LYSISTRATA.
  You *will*.

COMMISSIONER.
  What business have women with war and peace?

LYSISTRATA.
  I'll explain.

COMMISSIONER.
  I can hardly wait.

LYSISTRATA.
  Do stop clenching your fists. Do listen.

COMMISSIONER.
  That does it!

CHORUS B.
  Back!

COMMISSIONER.
  Who said that? Oh, you. Well, shut it.

  (*to* LYSISTRATA)

  Speak.

LYSISTRATA.
  All through this war, so far,
  We've sat there quietly and let you get on with it.
  Whether we agreed or not. Day after day after day,
  Whatever you chose to do, we were loyal wives,
  We didn't say a word. You went out in the morning,
  Sat with your men-friends in Assembly,   510
  Making Big Decisions (not Good, just Big) –
  And when you came home and we smiled and said,
  'Well darling, any news of peace today?',
  And you snarled and said, 'What's that to you?
  That's man-talk!', we left it alone, as good wives should.

CHORUS B.
  I didn't.

COMMISSIONER.
  God dammit, then leave it *now*!

LYSISTRATA.
Day after day after day. Whatever stupid news
Came back from the Assembly. I did once ask,
'Is that entirely sensible?' – and *he* said,
'Back to your weaving, unless you want a – !
520   Leave war to those who understand it: men.'

COMMISSIONER.
Sound fellow.

LYSISTRATA.
Sound? What a way to run a country!
Can't you hear them in the street? 'It's bad.
We're running out of manpower.' Dear, oh dear.
The solution's obvious: *woman* power.
And there's no time to waste. That's why we're
        here.
It's your turn to listen, and ours to talk.
Peace just may be women's business after all.

COMMISSIONER.
I'm not having this.

LYSISTRATA.
Of course you are.

COMMISSIONER.
530   Why should anyone listen to someone in a dress?

LYSISTRATA.
Is *that* what it is? That's easy.
Here, put this on. And this veil.
Take this shopping basket.
Now, roll up your sleeves,
Sit there, take this wool and these needles,
Get on with your knitting and *don't interrupt*.
Peace and war are feminine affairs.

CHORUS B.
Put down your water-jugs. It's our turn now.
540   It's time to take a stand and show them how.
Come leap, come sing, come dance.

Now, ladies! Seize your chance.
Don't yield, don't flinch,
Don't give an inch.
Be bold, be brash, be brave,
Athene's city save.
Bright victory dawns; her streamers streak the skies.
Up, daughters of the revolution! Rise!   550

LYSISTRATA.
Aphrodite, goddess of desire,
Eros, honey of the soul,
Breathe into our breasts and thighs
The dew of love, till our men strain ever upwards,
Till they call us Easers, Peace-makers,
Throughout all Greece.

COMMISSIONER.
Peace-makers? How?

LYSISTRATA.
By banning armour, for a start.
The market's no place to be flashing your hardware.

KALONIKE.
Amen to that.

LYSISTRATA.
All that clanking among the pots and pans –
Like some kind of strange religious sect.

COMMISSIONER.
Like brave men and true, you mean.

LYSISTRATA.
Brave men and true? Standing in line,
With shield and spear, to buy sardines?   560

MYRRHINE.
Like that dishy Captain I saw the other day...
Jingling his harness, tossing his hair,
While the soup-lady ladled his helmet.

KALONIKE.
> Or that Thracian – d'you remember? –
> Flaunting his snickersnack,
> Down at the fruit-stall, spearing six figs.

COMMISSIONER.
> And what about the international situation?
> How will you deal with that?

LYSISTRATA.
> Simplicity itself.

COMMISSIONER.
> Oh, do explain.

LYSISTRATA.
> When a bundle of wool is a tangle,
> We take it and tease it like *this*,
> And like *this*, and like *this*, till it's sorted.
> And that's just what we'll do with the war.
> Send ambassadors all over Greece,
> Disentangle and sort out the issues.

COMMISSIONER.
570
> Wool? Tangle? You're out of your minds.
> War's a serious business.

LYSISTRATA.
> I hadn't finished.

COMMISSIONER.
> So sorry. Do go on.

LYSISTRATA.
> Even when it's untangled, it has to be washed.
> In the same way, we'll see to the city.
> We'll lay it out on the carding-frame,
> Comb out the riff-raff, pick off the yes-men.
> Then whoever's left over goes into the basket:
580
> Citizens, visitors, strangers, tidy and neat.
> What about the colonies, the allies? Stray
>> threads,
> To be wound into one enormous ball of wool.

COMMISSIONER.
Colonies? Balls of wool?
I told you: women just can't get to grips with war.

LYSISTRATA.
Can't get to grips? Two agonies are ours:
We bear you sons, we wave goodbye when they
march to die.

COMMISSIONER.
Don't mention dying.   590

LYSISTRATA.
We're young, in the prime of life.
And what does war bring us? Single beds.
Bad enough for wives – but what about
Young girls, unmarried, doomed to die old
maids?

COMMISSIONER.
Don't men grow old?

LYSISTRATA.
Of course they do. But it isn't quite the same.
His Nibs comes home. He's toothless, grey –
But he'll still find a 'lassie' to marry him.
A woman's bloom is short, and when it fades,
No magician on Earth can conjure her a husband.

COMMISSIONER.
But if a man can still get it up –

LYSISTRATA.
You haven't heard a word I've said.
Ladies, he's dead. He's been dead for years –
To common sense. It's funeral time.   600
Here's rosemary...

She sprinkles him.

KALONIKE (*following suit*).
And rue.

MYRRHINE (*following suit*).
  Pansies. They're for thoughts.

CHORUS B.
  Weep, weep for Adonis,
  Too young, too young to die,
  To young in earth to lie.

COMMISSIONER.
  STOP IT! Ill-treating an officer of state!
  I'm off. I'll go like this. I'll show my colleagues.
  A dreadful warning. You've not heard the last of
610   this.

LYSISTRATA.
  And neither have you. We were only halfway
    through.
  We've wept for you and washed you.
  If you come back tomorrow, we'll dance on your
    grave.

  Exeunt.

CHORUS A.
  Fight, men of Athens, fight.
  There's evil in the air,
  It's everywhere,
  A smell of tyranny,
620   A smell of money, Spartan money,
  Corrupting our women, our wives,
  To rise against us, rise,
  Take what should be ours by right.

  Women! What do they know? 'Stop it!'
  'Beat those nasty swords to ploughshares!'
  'Talk to Sparta – do it nicely!'
  Talk to lions and wolves, more likely.
  Better yet, do what the song says:
630   'Face the foeman, fight for freedom,
  Save the city, trounce the tyrant,
  March, march, march, the men are marching...'

HUP, two, HUP, two – Who's that laughing?
You? I'll give you such a thrashing.

They dance and taunt the CHORUS OF OLD
WOMEN.

CHORUS B.

You, you old fool? You?
This way, ladies, this way.
It's time to speak,
Give sensible advice.
Who are we to advise the state?   640
At seven we danced in procession,
At eleven we led the cheers,
At twenty we danced, we danced.
And now you say we shouldn't meddle?
'Let your betters do the talking.'
What a brilliant job they're doing!
'War and peace – big issues, men's stuff.'   650
Human stuff! This race is *human*.
'Men pay tax. You don't contribute.'
All we give the state is children,
Son after son for slaughter. *You* spend!
Athens' hard-won wealth you squander!
Watch your mouth, or feel my slipper.

They dance and taunt the CHORUS OF OLD MEN.

CHORUS A.

Such impudence! Such insolence!
Who do you think you are?
It's now or never, gentlemen –   660
Come up and help. Strip off those cloaks,
Roll up your sleeves, make fists.
You are real men out there?
Comrades-in-arms?
Old soldiers?
Remember the good old days,
The good old fights.
Jump up here and help us now.   670

Stop these women! Wives and daughters!
Give an inch, they'll take advantage.
Launch a warship, sail against us,
Jolly Roger, splice the mainbrace,
Saddle horses, at the gallop,
Tally ho, they *do* love riding –
Amazons, she-devils, vampires.
Monsters out of children's stories,
Not to mention grown-ups' nightmares.

680   Grab them, men! The stocks are waiting.

Dance.

CHORUS B.

Just look at them! Such roars and threats!
Who do they think they are?
We'll show them, ladies. Up and help.
Strip off those cloaks, roll up your sleeves,
Sharp eyes, sharp nails, sharp teeth.
They really want a fight.
They're vinegar,

690   They're pepper.
Remember the fairy tale:
How that sweet little girl
Made hash of that Big Bad Wolf.

Huff and puff. Make scary faces.
Sparta's with us. Thebes is with us.
You've got no one. No one likes you.
Passing silly laws in council!

700   Yesterday I planned a party:
Eels from Thebes were on the menu –
Then the whole affair was cancelled.
'Enemy eels!' *you* said. 'No visa!'
Brains and common sense won't stop you –
Time for fists, and feet, and elbows.

Dance. Then enter LYSISTRATA.

CHORUS B.
   She comes. Our leader, counsellor, she comes.
   She's frowning. Leader, why? Why knit those brows?

LYSISTRATA.
   I'm quite distraught. I don't know what to do.

CHORUS B.
   My god! My god!   710

LYSISTRATA.
   It's true! It's true!

CHORUS B.
   What is it? Tell your friends. Vouchsafe.

LYSISTRATA.
   Vouchsafe? I shudder. Nay, I blench.

CHORUS B.
   Enough Euripides. What's going on?

LYSISTRATA.
   It's simple. We'll never hold out.
   We're dying – for a fuck.

CHORUS B.
   O Zeus!

LYSISTRATA.
   What's Zeus to do with it? It's men they want.
   They won't stay put. They're slipping out: this way
   That way – I caught one in Pan's Grotto, tunnelling. 720
   There were two on the battlements just now.
   One was abseiling. The other was gathering sparrows:
   Something about holding their legs and floating down
   To pay an urgent call. We all know where.
   If I hadn't grabbed her hair, she'd be there now.
   They've a hundred excuses, but one destination: bed.
   Here's someone now.

   The DEFECTOR *creeps out.*

   Ahem!

DEFECTOR.
    I must get home.
    I bought some lovely wool the other day,
    And the bugs are at it.

LYSISTRATA.
    What bugs?

DEFECTOR.
730   Bed-bugs.
    I want to stretch it on the bed, and scratch.
    I won't be long.

LYSISTRATA.
    No stretching. No scratching. Stay.

DEFECTOR.
    But what about my wool?

LYSISTRATA.
    Forget your wool.

    KALONIKE *comes out*.

KALONIKE.
    My dough! My dough! I need to knead my dough!

LYSISTRATA.
    Your dough doesn't need kneading, and neither do
      you.

KALONIKE.
    But it'll rise, dear, rise till it explodes.
    I'll give it a little knead, and come right back.

LYSISTRATA.
740   No kneading, no coming. If I let *you* go,
    They'll all start baking.

    Enter MYRRHINE.

MYRRHINE.
    I've got to go. Quick!
    I *can't*...not here. Not in a sacred place.

LYSISTRATA.
  Not what?

MYRRHINE.
  Give birth. The pains have started. Look.

LYSISTRATA.
  You weren't even pregnant yesterday.

MYRRHINE.
  I am today.
  Oh, please, Lysistrata, I must get home.
  The midwife's waiting. There it goes again!

LYSISTRATA.
  What nonsense! Just a minute. What *is* that bulge?

MYRRHINE.
  A darling baby boy.

LYSISTRATA.
  What d'you mean? It's hard.
  It's hollow. It's Athene's golden helmet.   750
  You said you were pregnant.

MYRRHINE.
  I am, I am.

LYSISTRATA.
  So why the helmet?

MYRRHINE.
  In case the baby comes too soon. Before I get home.
  A cradle. That's what it is. A holy cradle.

LYSISTRATA.
  What's happened to your lump?

MYRRHINE.
  Ooh! Gone. A false alarm.
  How strange! I've been dreaming of snakes
  For *weeks*.

KALONIKE.
  At least you can sleep up here. I can't.

760   Owls hooting all the time. Athene's owls.
      It's scary.

LYSISTRATA.
     Owls? Snakes? Don't you understand?
     It's *men* you're thinking of. And that is *good*.
     If *you* want *them*, *they* must be dying for *you*.
     Sleepless nights. Just a few more days.
     I know it's hard, but just a few more days.
     The oracle said –

DEFECTOR.
     What oracle?

LYSISTRATA.
     LO! WHEN THE SWALLOWS COME
       SWOOPING, SWOOPING,
     LO! WHEN THEY FLOCK FROM THE
770   HOOPOE, HOOPOE,
     THEN WILL THE UPSY BE DOWNSY, THE
       DOWNSY UPSY –

KALONIKE.
     We go on top...?

LYSISTRATA.
     LO! IF THE SWALLOWS START FLAPPING
       AND FLOCKING,
     LO! IF THEY SPEED FROM THEIR NEST ON
       THE BATTLEMENTS,
     KEEKERY, COCKERY, MUD THEN THEIR
       NAME WILL BE.

MYRRHINE.
     Wow! What an oracle!

KALONIKE.
     Merciful Heaven!

LYSISTRATA.
     We must do what it says. Don't you see?
780   We must go inside, do exactly what it says.

She ushers them in.

CHORUS A.
I've a tale to tell, from Greek mythology:
Sheds a blinding light on male psychology.
I've known it for years.
Are you ready, dears?
It's about Melanion (not the marrying kind),
And his would-be in-laws (the harrying kind).
They pester; off he streaks,
Changes his habits;
Holes up in the peaks;
Hunts rabbits;   790
Never seen again.
That's how women take some men.
He got away. Refused to take the strain –
And if *we'd* any sense, we'd do the same.

OLD MAN.
Hey, kiss me quick.

OLD WOMAN.
That's silly.

OLD MAN.
You prefer a kick?

OLD WOMAN.
Your willy!   800

OLD MAN.
Too shaggy?
Too baggy?
It knows what to do.
It'll soon see to you.

Dance.

CHORUS B.
I've a tale to tell, from ancient history –
Well, not so much a tale, more of a mystery.
What, solve it? No one can:
It's typical man.

It's about Timon of Athens (a tragic case),
810   And his loathing of (half) the human race.
Always frowning, always scowling,
Muttering and groaning,
Rumbling and growling
And moaning.
Men *always* made him curse,
He could think of nothing worse –
You'd have thought all the male sex had rabies.
820   Only males, mind. He still liked the ladies.

OLD WOMAN.
A stamp on the toes?

OLD MAN.
I'm going.

OLD WOMAN.
A boot up the nose?

OLD MAN.
You're showing.

OLD WOMAN.
So what, Dad?
It's not bad.
It's properly behaved.
It's not like yours: it's shaved.

Dance. As it ends, LYSISTRATA *comes out*[28].

LYSISTRATA.
Women! Women! Quick!

Enter KALONIKE, MYRRHINE *and* WOMEN.

KALONIKE.
830   What is it? Why are you shouting, dear?

LYSISTRATA.
Look, a man! Look at the state he's in.
All geared up for the rites of Aphrodite.
Great goddess, lady of Paphos, of Kythera,
Help us! Make sure he isn't up to it.

KALONIKE.
  Where is he, this man?

LYSISTRATA.
  Down there, by Chloe's temple.

KALONIKE.
  So he is. Who d'you think he is?

LYSISTRATA.
  Don't any of you recognise him?

MYRRHINE.
  Ooh yes, I do.
  It's my husband. Kinesias.

LYSISTRATA.
  Your husband. Good. You know what to do.
  Let him get as far as the entrance, but NO FURTHER.
  Get him twisting and wriggling and foaming,
  Flirt with him, kiss him, offer him everything,   840
  But NO ENTRY.

MYRRHINE.
  If you say so.

LYSISTRATA.
  Don't worry. I'll be here. I'll help you.
  Between us we'll work him up to bursting point.
  The rest of you, quickly, out of sight.

  The WOMEN *go in, except for* LYSISTRATA.
  Enter KINESIAS, *with a* SLAVE *holding his*
  BABY.

KINESIAS.
  Drooping and shaking,
  Quivering and quaking,
  An itch without a scratch,
  A hole without a patch,
  I'm done for, stretched and aching –

LYSISTRATA.
 Who goes there? These parts are private.
 What are you, coming here in that condition?

KINESIAS.
 You can see what I am.

LYSISTRATA.
 A man?

KINESIAS.
 Look, dammit!

LYSISTRATA.
 Withdraw at once!

KINESIAS.
 Who are you to tell me to withdraw?

LYSISTRATA.
 I watch the gate.

KINESIAS.
850 Never mind the gate. Call Myrrhine.

LYSISTRATA.
 Why should I?

KINESIAS.
 Because I'm her husband. Kinesias.
 Mine's a sad tale...

LYSISTRATA.
 Oh, we know all about your tail.
 Myrrhine's told us all about your tail.
 You're never out of her mouth.
 Give her an apple or an egg to hold, and she's off:
 'So smooth and round...I'd like to give it to
 Kinesias...'

KINESIAS.
 Oh gods.

LYSISTRATA.
 I promise you. No one else dare mention

Her husband round here, or Myrrhine says,
  'Broken reed! Blunt pencil, compared to mine.'   860

KINESIAS.
  Oh, call her, call her.

LYSISTRATA.
  You still haven't said: why should I?

KINESIAS.
  Oh god. How long d'you expect me to keep this up?
  I'll squeeze you something later. *Call* her. Please.

LYSISTRATA.
  Excuse me a moment.

  She goes in.

KINESIAS.
  Hurry.

  (*to the* BABY)

  She's no idea what it's like, since Mummy left.
  Life's not life any more. Going in, going out,
  I ache, I thirst, I pine. Not to mention *this*.

MYRRHINE (*off*).
  Tell him I love him, dear *sweet* man,   870
  But he keeps putting something between us.
  It's no use asking, darling. I won't come down.

KINESIAS.
  Myrrhine, sweetheart, why, oh why, oh why?
  Don't torture me. Come down.

  MYRRHINE *appears*[29].

MYRRHINE.
  Shan't.

KINESIAS.
  But it's me, sweetheart. Won't you come, for me?

MYRRHINE.
  I can't think what you want me for.

KINESIAS.
It sticks out a mile.

MYRRHINE.
I'm going.

KINESIAS.
No. Listen to Diddums.

(*to the* BABY)

Call Mummy. Call her, dammit.

BABY.
Mammeea, mammeea, mammeea.

KINESIAS.
880   There you are. Poor little devil. Six days now,
Not one nappy-change, not a *suck* of milk...

MYRRHINE.
Poor little boy. Has Daddy been neglecting oo?

KINESIAS.
Please come. Please come for Diddums.

MYRRHINE.
Oh, motherhood! I'll have to come.
There's no alternative.

She makes a proper entrance.

KINESIAS.
Oh, look at her, *look* at her.
Mummy's cwoss with Daddikins. Such fwowns.
I can't stand it. I can't *stand* it.

MYRRHINE (*to the* BABY).
Poor darling. There, there.
Has Daddy been nasty to oo again?
890   Come to Mummy. There, there, there.

KINESIAS.
What are you playing at? Going off
With that pack of silly women, and leaving me...
Leaving me... What's got into you?

MYRRHINE.
Don't touch me.

KINESIAS.
But everything's gone to seed since you left home.

MYRRHINE.
Don't care.

KINESIAS.
That knitting, that lovely knitting you were doing.
Gone! In the night! A flock of roosters ate it.

MYRRHINE.
Don't care.

KINESIAS.
Don't you remember? The plans we made?
Just you and I? Our own little Olympic Games?

MYRRHINE.
There'll be no Olympic Games, till you get   900
That treaty signed.

KINESIAS.
Treaty? Oh, treaty. Anything!

MYRRHINE.
Sign that, and I'll come right home.
Till then, excuse me.

KINESIAS.
Don't go. I'll sign.
Couldn't you...? Can't we...? Just a little...?

MYRRHINE.
Sorry. Though I must say I'm tempted.

KINESIAS.
You are? You must? Oh darling, *now*.

MYRRHINE.
You filthy beast! In front of Diddums?

KINESIAS.
Oh my god, Diddums.

(*to the* SLAVE)

Here, man, here. Get him out of here.

Exit SLAVE *with* BABY.

He's gone, darling, gone. Now, come to bed.

MYRRHINE.
910   Bed? Where?

KINESIAS.
Where? Um... Pan's Grotto!

MYRRHINE.
It's dusty, darling. Where can I wash?

KINESIAS.
In the fountain. Do come on.

MYRRHINE.
But what about my oath? I swore an oath.

KINESIAS.
Blame me. *I* broke it. Hurry up.

MYRRHINE.
I'll just fetch a bed.

KINESIAS.
What? On the ground, the ground.

MYRRHINE.
No, darling. You may be a pig,
But I won't let you wallow on the ground.

She goes in.

KINESIAS.
She loves me. She loves me. You can always tell.

MYRRHINE *returns with a folding bed.*

MYRRHINE.
You set it up. I'll get undressed.
No, silly me. I forgot the mattress.

KINESIAS.
   Forget the mattress.

MYRRHINE.
   I can't have you having me on sacking.   920

KINESIAS.
   Give me a kiss before you go.

MYRRHINE.
   Mmmmmmmmmmmm.

   She goes in.

KINESIAS.
   Hoo-hoo-hoo. For god's sake hurry.

   MYRRHINE *returns with a mattress.*

MYRRHINE.
   There. You lie down. I'll get undressed.
   Oh no. No pillow, now.

KINESIAS.
   I don't *want* a pillow.

MYRRHINE.
   But I do.

   She goes.

KINESIAS.
   What do I look like? Herakles. Complete with club.

   MYRRHINE *comes back with a pillow.*

MYRRHINE.
   Get your head up.

KINESIAS.
   It is up.

MYRRHINE.
   Everything's ready, then.

KINESIAS.
   Come on then, sweetheart.   930

MYRRHINE.
Just coming. I don't want to crease this dress.
All that about the treaty just now...
You weren't just having me on?

KINESIAS.
Having you? Oh, *on*. Of course not.

MYRRHINE.
Brr! No blanket.

KINESIAS.
I don't want a blanket, I want you.

MYRRHINE.
Won't be a moment.

She goes in.

KINESIAS.
Man dies on Acropolis, in broad daylight,
Smothered in bedclothes!

MYRRHINE *comes back with a blanket.*

MYRRHINE.
Upsadaisy.

KINESIAS.
Don't keep *saying* that.

MYRRHINE.
Would you like me to rub you with scented oil?

KINESIAS.
No!

MYRRHINE.
Of course I will. Don't be so grumpy.

She fetches a flask of oil.

KINESIAS.
940   Pour it on, then.

MYRRHINE.
No, no: *you*. Hold out your hand.

KINESIAS.
  Apollo, how I hate perfumed oil.
  And especially perfumed oil that smells like *this*.

MYRRHINE.
  What d'you mean? Did I bring the wrong one?

KINESIAS.
  No. No! It's lovely. Wait.

MYRRHINE.
  No trouble.

  She goes in.

KINESIAS.
  God damn the man who invented perfumed oil.

  MYRRHINE *comes back with another flask. It is*
  phallus-shaped.

MYRRHINE.
  This is *much* nicer. Look.

KINESIAS.
  Blunt pencil, compared to mine.
  Do stop rushing about, and come and lie down.

MYRRHINE.
  In a moment. In a moment.
  I've still to take this off.
  Darling, you *will* do what you said?   950
  Bring it up...peace...in the Assembly?

KINESIAS.
  I'll think about it.

  MYRRHINE *goes.*

  Now what is it? What's the matter?
  She's gone. She came, and fetched, and went.
  The most beautiful girl in the world.
  Leaving me like this. Leaving *you* like this.
  What shall I do with you now?
  I know what you need. I know, I *know*.

What's the name of that...establishment...down the
road?

CHORUS A.
Weep and moan,
960   Grieve and groan.
You're the unluckiest man alive.
How *will* you survive?
A-ee, a-ee.
What can we say?
Just think what you're missing:
No petting, no kissing,
No getting your end away.

KINESIAS.
Alack! I'm on the rack.

CHORUS A.
And she's to blame
They're all the same.

KINESIAS.
970   Adorable.

CHORUS A.
Deplorable.

KINESIAS.
Oh what's the use?
Please, Zeus,
Pluck her, suck her
High, in the sky,
Then drop her down again,
Kinesias begs –
Take careful aim –
Between these legs.

Dance. Exit KINESIAS. *Enter* SPARTAN
MESSENGER.

MESSENGER[27].
    Excuse me. People of Athens? Councillors?   980
    Anyone in? There's something I want to raise.

    Enter DOORKEEPER.

DOORKEEPER.
    There certainly is. What are you, man or teapot?

MESSENGER.
    A messenger, lassie, with a message.
    From the Commonwealth of Sparta. About a peace.

DOORKEEPER.
    Peace? With a spear like that?

MESSENGER.
    Spear? What spear?

DOORKEEPER.
    Oh, I'm sorry. It's the way you hold your cloak.
    Is it *very* sore?

MESSENGER.
    What are you talking about?

DOORKEEPER.
    Don't tell me you're just glad to see me.

MESSENGER.
    Don't be so cheeky.   990

DOORKEEPER.
    What is it, then?

MESSENGER.
    Rod of office. Rod of iron.

DOORKEEPER.
    I've heard about your Spartan rods of iron.

    Enter COMMISSIONER.

COMMISSIONER.
    What is it you want? You can tell me.
    Speak up. How are things in Sparta?

MESSENGER.
> How *are* things? They *aren't*.
> And our allies are getting damned uptight.
> Take things into their own hands,
> If we don't look out.

COMMISSIONER.
> Explain yourself.

MESSENGER.
> In one word: Lampito. Going A.W.O.L. at lights-out.
1000
> Then all the other women followed suit.
> Barriers up, drawbridges closed. Frustrating.

COMMISSIONER.
> So what are *you* doing? You men?

MESSENGER.
> What d'you think? Going round, bent double:
> You'd think we were carrying candles in a gale.
> They stand there, laugh, won't shake their
>   blossoms
> Till we make some kind of universal peace.

COMMISSIONER.
> It's a conspiracy. They're all in this.
> Every woman in Greece. *Now* I understand.
> Look, we're in their hands. No time to lose.
1010
> Go back to Sparta, tell them to send a mission.
> I'll see to this end. If you have any trouble,
> Do what I do when the Assembly asks awkward
>   questions:
> Lift up your tunic and show them your evidence.

MESSENGER.
> Anything. If it brings relief.

> *Exeunt.*

CHORUS A.
> Women! Hot as fire – no, hotter;
> Fierce as tigers – no, far fiercer –

CHORUS B.
Daft old fool. You chose to fight us.
Knew all that and chose to fight us.

CHORUS A.
Course I did. I hate all women.

CHORUS B.
If you say so. Look, you're shaking.
Standing there all soaked and shaking.   1020
Daft old fool! Here, let me help you.

CHORUS A.
No one fights and keeps his cloak on,
Growls and roars and keeps his cloak on.

CHORUS B.
Course they don't. That's better. There, now.
What's the matter? Do stand still, man.
Something in your eye? An insect?

CHORUS A.
Damn mosquito, buzzing, biting,
Swimming round beside my eyeball.
Don't just stand there. Ow! Be careful!

CHORUS B.
Manners! Goodness, what a monster!   1030
No mosquito, more a hornet.

CHORUS A.
Thanks. It nearly gouged my eye out.
Eyes are running. Can't stop crying.

CHORUS B.
Let me wipe it. Kiss it better –

CHORUS A.
Not in front of all these people.

CHORUS B.
Do as Mummy says. Don't argue.

CHORUS A.
Women! Always have to get your own way.

Twist us round your little finger.
Can't live with 'em, can't ignore 'em.
1040 Let's stop fighting. Come to Daddy.
Hand in hand. That's right. Let's dance now.

Dance. From now on, CHORUS A *and* CHORUS B
are united.

CHORUS.
Smile, ladies and gentlemen.
Those happy days *are* here again.
Malice and insults? No, no, no:
This Chorus turns its back on woe.
What d'you mean, 'Big deal'?
I'll tell you how I feel.
1050 Who needs a loan? Yes? You, sir?
I'll tell you what to do, sir.
Once peace is signed
I think you'll find
You needn't pay back – don't ask me how –
One penny of the cash I lend you now.

Now, dear friends, before you go,
There's a party after the show.
Rowdy and hearty? Rude and loud?
1060 Of course not. An upmarket crowd.
Good food? Not half –
A fatted calf.
Who wants to come? Yes? You?
I'll tell you exactly what to do.
Take a bath, dress smart –
You've got to look the part –
1070 Then hurry back as if you owned the place,
And find the door slammed in your face.

Dance.

Here come the ambassadors from Sparta.
What are those things between their legs?
I took my pussy to the vet in one of those.

Enter the SPARTAN AMBASSADOR, *attended.*

Good sirs of Sparta, welcome. How now? What
  cheer?

AMBASSADOR.
What d'you mean, what cheer? *This* cheer.

CHORUS.
I see the problem. Getting bigger all the time.
Too much of a strain. Something's got to give.

AMBASSADOR.
Spare the diagnosis. Make the peace.   1080

CHORUS.
Here's *our* delegation. Something's up here as well.
It's an epidemic. Does *everyone* walk like that?

Enter an ATHENIAN CITIZEN.

CITIZEN.
Someone fetch Lysistrata, at once.
We can't go on like this.

CHORUS.
It *is* an epidemic. Do you shake before breakfast?

CITIZEN.
It's drastic. If something doesn't happen soon,   1090
I wouldn't like to be Kleisthenes, that's all.

CHORUS.
Put your cloak straight, for Heaven's sake.
Remember what happened to all those Herms?[230]
Every one got the chop.

CITIZEN.
Don't remind me.

AMBASSADOR.
What is all this? What chop?
Ah, that chop. Cloaks, chaps, NOW.

Enter COMMISSIONER.

COMMISSIONER.
  Your Excellency. Gentlemen. Hard times.

AMBASSADOR.
  I wish people wouldn't keep *saying* that.

COMMISSIONER.
1100 Well, gentlemen, down to business.
  What brings you here?

AMBASSADOR.
  We want to talk peace.

COMMISSIONER.
  Well, so do we.
  I think we ought to call Lysistrata.
  She'll sort it out.

AMBASSADOR.
  For god's sake call her, then.

CHORUS.
  No need. She must have heard. She's here.

  Enter LYSISTRATA.

COMMISSIONER.
  Lysistrata, good man. Er...

CHORUS.
  It's time, now. Time to be
  Hard...
  Soft...
  Enterprising...
  Thoughtful...
  Persuasive...
  Accessible...
  All things to all men.
1110 All men are here: the whole of Greece.
  They're in your hands. It's up to you. Speak now!

LYSISTRATA.
  It won't be hard, if they're ready to shake hands

Instead of going for one another's throats.
We'll soon find out. Bring Reconciliation.

As she continues, RECONCILIATION *is fetched in.*

Bring the Spartans over here. Handle them gently,
Like ladies, not rudely, roughly,
The way our husbands do.
That's right, take their hands.
Those *are* their hands?
Now, fetch the Athenians.   1120
Over here. That's right.
They want their 'hands' held too.
Now, gentlemen.
Stand straight and listen.
I may be a woman, but I'm not a fool.
My father, my elders – I've listened to them all,
And I know what I think. It's this.
You ought to be ashamed. All of you.
We're all Greeks here. One family.   1130
Thermopylai, Delphi, the Olympic Games –
I could go on. One heritage, the same for all.
And still, with the enemy all but at the gates,
Greek turns on Greek. You're like mice,
      squabbling
While the cat sits waiting. Point Number One.

COMMISSIONER.
   Have you *seen* that girlie?

LYSISTRATA.
   Sparta first. D'you remember that slave revolt,
   Just after the earthquake, not so long ago?
   The Messenian business? The trouble you were in?
   What was his name, that ambassador
   You sent up here for help? Perikleides.
   Bright red cloak, white face, begging for soldiers.   1140
   And out we marched, Kimon, four thousand men,
   Saved Sparta's bacon and marched right back again.
   We did that for you, and what do you do for us?
   You invade us, plunder us: make war on family.

COMMISSIONER.
  Lysistrata, you tell 'em.

AMBASSADOR.
  What a behind. Er...what a good point.

LYSISTRATA.
  Athens next. You're just as bad.
  Have you forgotten Hippias,
  When he tried to sweep away democracy
  With a gang of thugs from Thessaly?
1150 D'you remember how Sparta rode to the rescue,
  A rattle of shields, a storm of spears,
  All over in a morning, rule of law preserved?
  That's what Sparta did. Think about it.
  If it hadn't been for Sparta,
  What would you be now?
  Not free men, not democrats, but slaves.

  The men are still gaping at RECONCILIATION.

AMBASSADOR.
  She has got a point.

COMMISSIONER.
  You should see from here.

LYSISTRATA.
  We're family. We're friends. We *owe* each other.
1160 Why are we fighting? What's your opinion, sir?

AMBASSADOR.
  What a fantastic pair of – ah, conditions.
  Conditions, before we agree.

LYSISTRATA.
  What conditions?

AMBASSADOR.
  Pylos³¹. These narrows, here.
  Strategic importance. We have to have them.

COMMISSIONER.
  No chance.

LYSISTRATA.
  Oh, let them have them.

COMMISSIONER.
  And what do we get?

LYSISTRATA.
  Name it.

COMMISSIONER.
  This area. From the peaks up here
  To the scrubland here...   1170

AMBASSADOR.
  You're joking.

LYSISTRATA.
  Don't fight for a bit of scrub.

COMMISSIONER.
  My plans include stripping, ploughing...

AMBASSADOR.
  I've a fertilisation scheme in mind.

LYSISTRATA.
  Why not make peace...and *share*?
  If that's agreed, shake hands here now
  And then put it to the allies.

COMMISSIONER.
  Don't worry about the allies. Whatever we put up,
  They'll ram it home like the gallant lads they are.

AMBASSADOR.
  So will ours. No flabbiness down there.   1180

COMMISSIONER.
  Karystos' all set.[32]

LYSISTRATA.
  Right. Go inside and sacrifice.
  We'll go back home, get the party ready.
  When you've sworn your oaths,

When you've promised to be good,
We'll be waiting to welcome you with open arms.

COMMISSIONER.
Come on, this way.

AMBASSADOR.
No, after you.

COMMISSIONER.
Get on with it!

Exeunt all but CHORUS.

CHORUS.
Bedspreads and blankets and sheets crispy-white;
1190   Necklaces, bracelets and rings shiny-bright;
All of them free,
Waiting for *you*.
Just form a queue –
And whatever you see,
Jar of fresh water,
Dress for your daughter –
Stroke it and pat it,
1200   Grab it and nab it –
Just be sure that I don't catch you at it.

Pastries and tartlets and slices of cake;
Breadrolls and bloomers and baps from the bake;
Just what you need
For your kiddies, your wife;
Bring a fork; bring a knife,
If you fancy a feed.
Look at the menu,
1210   Order, and then you
Can feast like a hog,
Lunching and munching –
There's just one thing: Beware of the Dog.

Dance. When it ends, the COMMISSIONER *and his retinue come out of the central doorway, drunk and with torches.*

COMMISSIONER.
  This way. Mind the door. Whoops!
  Why are you lying there in heaps?
  Want me to singe your bums for you?

  (*to the audience*)

  I shouldn't be doing this. You shouldn't be watching.
  It's vulgar. What d'you mean, you're enjoying it?
  Oh well, whatever the public wants.   1220

ATHENIAN CITIZEN.
  Wharreverapublicwants.

COMMISSIONER.
  Move, I said. Layabouts. Stir yourselves.
  Our guests are on their way. Home from dinner.
  We don't want them stumbling over riff-raff.

CITIZEN.
  Proper gents. Thass what *they* are. Gents.
  Did you see them drinking? Hollow legs.
  Mind you, we din do so bad ourselves.

COMMISSIONER.
  Of course we dint. Take it from me:
  If you don drink, stay out of politics.   1230
  Thass what politicians need: big drinks.
  I mean, you know what we're like when we're sober:
  Yap yap, nag nag, row row. And afterwards –
  Your head's like a wrung-out sponge;
  You seem to remember something...what?
  Total disaster. But when you've had a few, like now:
  Everyone smiling, everyone clapping an cheering,
  Sing us the old songs, give us another.
  Shh! They're coming. Our friends. Our guests.
  Get out of the way. We don't want riff-raff.   1240

CITIZEN.
  Gerrout of the way. They wanna dance.

  Enter AMBASSADOR *and* SPARTANS.

AMBASSADOR.
> Where's the piper? Squeeze that bag, man.
> I feel like dancing, like singing.
> For all our friends in Athens. And at home.

CITIZEN.
> Yeah, baggy, give's a blow.
> I wanna watchim dance.

Music. Dance[33].

SPARTAN(S).
> Sing, Memory.
> Bring the old days alive again,
> The good old days.
1250   Sing of valour, of victory,
> How Athens sent a cloud,
> A storm of ships
> To sink the Persians;
> How Sparta sent hunters,
> Boar-hunters,
> To trap the beast in blood.
> Persians, countless,
> Numberless as sand,
1260   Sweating, running.

> Come, Artemis.
> Lady, huntress, come to us, come,
> Smile on us, smile.
> All arguments over, we smile,
> Shake hands, make peace.
> Huntress, come,
> Your dogs, your spears,
> Smile on us,
> End wrangles that eat the soul,
> Gnawing, tearing.
> Sweet lady, come to us,
> Dance with us,
1270   Sweet lady, smile[34].

LYSISTRATA.
All's well that ends well. Spartans, dance.
People of Athens, seize your chance.
Now wife with husband, man with wife,
Step lively in the dance of life.
Pray blessings. May they never cease.
Quiet lives, good sense, unending peace.

ATHENIAN(S).
Graces, dance.
Artemis, dance.   1280
Apollo, lead the dance.
Dionysos, your Maenads, dance.
Zeus, lord of lightning,
Dance.
Hera, queen of Heaven,
Dance.
Gods above,
Dance for us,
Dance for our happiness,
Dance for our joy,   1290
Ee-a-ee,
Happiness,
Ee-a-ee,
Yoo-o-ee, yoo-o-ee, yoo-a-ee, yoo-a-ee.

LYSISTRATA.
Now your turn. A Spartan song.

SPARTAN(S).
From high hills echoing,
Sing, Muse of Sparta, sing.
Sing Apollo, Athene sing,   1300
Sing Castor, Pollux sing.
By the waters of Sparta sing.
E-ee-a,
Girls of Sparta, sing,
Dancing, foals,
A whirl,
A stampede,   1310

Manes flying,
Dance by the riverside,
For Dionysos, Dionysos,
Dance.
Daughter of Leda, dance!

Whirl, leap, spin, twirl.
Hair streaming, cymbals, pounding feet,
1320   Dance for the goddess, dance for peace.

Exeunt omnes.

NOTES

Acharnians

1. Scholars have teased out this gibberish in two ways. In old Persian it (almost) means, 'The king told me he was sending gold.' In old Sanskrit (!) it (almost) means, 'Xerxes sent me here for nothing.'

2. The scene which follows parodies the Rural Dionysia: a small-scale blessing of fields and farms which took place either at vine-dressing or grape-harvesting time. Very little is known about it – in fact, in a neat circular situation, this scene is the main ancient evidence for what went on – but processions, hymns and phallic ribaldry seem safe bets.

3. Part of the joke in the scenes which follow – not to mention the hostage scene just past – comes from Aristophanes' constant references to Euripides' tragedy *Telephos* (now lost). In myth, the Greeks who sailed to recapture Helen of Troy made their first landfall in pro-Trojan Mysia (the eastern coast of the Sea of Marmara). In the fight which followed, Achilles wounded the Mysian king, Telephos. The Greeks sailed on to Troy – and the gods told Telephos that only 'the wounder' would heal him. He sailed after the Greeks, went into their camp disguised as a lame beggar, and stole Agamemnon's infant son Orestes, holding him hostage until the Greeks listened to his appeal for help. In due course, it was discovered that Achilles' spear was the mysterious 'wounder', and rust from it cured Telephos' injury. Euripides' play on this theme was first performed in 438BC, a dozen years before *Acharnians*. Aristophanes later parodied the *Telephos* hostage scene (along with many other Euripides scenes) in *Festival Time*. That passage, and this one here, contain several lines apparently quoted directly from the play. Otherwise, in this scene, Euripides, Kephisophon and Dikaiopolis speak a mixture of ordinary dialogue, theatre slang, in-jokes, quotations and reminiscences of

tragedy – the tone and style of which I have rendered in modern terms.

4. The staging of what follows depends on how one interprets the Greek words *ekkuklein* ('roll out') and *anabaden* ('up'). Euripides says he will not come down, and Dikaiopolis suggests that he should have himself 'rolled out'. Some scholars say that this refers to a wheeled sofa, a device sometimes used in tragedy to bring forward the corpses of people killed 'within'; others that it refers to scenery screens which could be wheeled away. The result is that Euripides is discovered to be (in Dikaiopolis' words) 'composing – up'. Some take this to mean on an upper level; others with his feet up; others with his phallus erect.

5. In the original, Aristophanes makes the Megarians steal whores from the 'house of Aspasia'. It was a well-worn joke that Aspasia, mistress of Athens' great leader Perikles, ran a brothel on the side. Perikles, whose own nickname was 'The Olympian' (i.e. 'Zeus') passed the Megarian Decree in 432BC, thus precipitating the war with Sparta (though not, one imagines, for the reasons given by Aristophanes here), and died in 429BC, four years before *Acharnians*.

6. In Greek, the Megarian and Theban are dialect parts. One of the underlying jokes in the Megarian scene – enhancing the political point about Megarian desperation – is that 'pig', in Athenian slang, meant 'cunt'.

7. The original puns on the words *diapeinomen* ('We're starving to death'), which the Megarian actually says, and *diapinomen* ('We're drinking to death'), which Dikaiopolis pretends to hear.

8. In Greek, there was an extra layer to the sequence which follows: *ischas* ('dried fig') was also slang for a wrinkled, flaccid penis.

9. In the original, the invitation came from the Priest of Dionysos, in whose theatre and in front of whose shrine the performance was taking place. As you went off-stage

in the theatre, you would have walked down towards the priest's living-quarters at the corner of the shrine.

10. One of the oldest traditions of Greek comedy was insult, usually rude, shouted after processions of Dionysos. This survives in Aristophanes: short passages about specific individuals, whose characters and misfortunes usually have nothing to do with the main action. Here the butt is Aristophanes' own former backer – and the jokes against him are probably no more serious than a modern comedian's mockery of (say) his agent.

Knights

11. Like Paphlagon/Kleon, the Rope-knotter (literally, seller-of-hemp) and sheep-seller were real politicians: Eukrates and Lysikrates. Topicality apart, the point of the joke is that each has a lower and more degrading job than the last.

12. This undramatic disappearance may be because the play was originally performed with only three actors, and the actor who played Nikias had to change into another mask and costume, ready to come on as Paphlagon on page 76.

13. The Knights were a thousand young men from wealthy families, who formed an élite group of officers in the cavalry. They were known for their spectacular turn-out at processions and festivals, especially the huge Panathenaic Festival in July, when they paraded through the city on horseback and in magnificent ceremonial uniforms.

14. The first section of the *parabasis* (address to the audience) which follows deals with theatrical matters. Although plays by Aristophanes had been performed before, *Knights* was the first to be produced in his own name. He explains why, in a passage referring

affectionately to older rivals: Magnes, Kratinos and Krates. The other two speeches (interspersed with hymns for victory to Poseidon, patron god of the Knights, and Athene, protectress of Athens) concern the real-life Knights themselves. The first talks of their proud traditions (including, at the end, long curly hair and warm baths, which some people took for signs of effeminacy). The second refers to a recent cavalry expedition against Corinth. In Aristophanes' version the Knights' horses are credited with all the effort; a more historical account is given in Thoukydides' *History*, Book 4 chapters 42ff. For the Greek audience, two jokes would have had extra point: the by-now standard references to Aristophanes' premature baldness, and the one about crabs at the end. 'Crab' seems to have been a slang word for Corinthian, like 'Frog' for Frenchman in Victorian English. Corinth, too, was famous in comedy as the brothel capital of Greece, and 'crab' is slang for prostitute.

15. In the original, the action of the play takes place on the Pnyx hill, the place for democratic gatherings of the whole Athenian people.

16. The story of Pylos is outlined in the introduction (pages xxiv–xxv). After the victory, the captured Spartan shields were publicly displayed in the *agora*, and preserved with great care – one of them was found, in a recognizable condition, by modern archaeologists twenty-four centuries later. Normally shields displayed in this way had their handles removed – hence the panic Demos feels at Agorakritos' next suggestion.

17. Underlying the dialogue about shoes and poofs is a complex piece of *double entendre*. Wearing shoes, in Athenian slang, was a synonym for sexual intercourse, particularly homosexual; it is also a standard Aristophanic metaphor that the way politicians treat the people is a form of buggery.

18. The remaining dishes, in Greek, consist of a stream of puns with religious or political themes. The dishes and jokes without the puns (impossible to reproduce in English) make little sense, and I have accordingly slightly shortened the passage in translation.

Peace

19. I have borrowed this happy wordplay from Patric Dickinson's translation (OUP 1957), page 225. The original means, 'Give him another, from a prostituted boy. He says he likes them ready rubbed.'

20. Original: a mortar. But the subsequent dialogue about pestles and cooking ingredients would nowadays seem obscure. I have therefore replaced the metaphor of War's kitchen with one of War's smithy, throughout. (In the original metaphor, War throws into a huge mortar ingredients consisting of the chief exports of certain cities: leeks for Prasiai, garlic for Megara, cheese for Sicily and honey for the Athenian region. He sends Quarrel to Earth in search of a pestle to grind them all together.)

21. Original: 'to quote the tune Datis sang as he jerked himself off in the afternoon.'

22. Original: 'He's turned into Simonides in his old age – if you paid him enough, he'd go to sea in a sieve.' The point of this is unclear.

23. It is possible that in the Greek production, he and the girls went out at one side, and reappeared at the other. This parallels Xanthias' long walk, in similar circumstances, when he is not allowed to sail in Charon's boat in *Frogs*.

24. There follows the *parabasis*, praising Aristophanes and disparaging his rivals. Part of it (lines 752ff) is repeated, almost exactly, from the *parabasis* of *Wasps* –

as are the later references to Aristophanes' premature baldness. There are interpretative problems in lines 775ff, whose main claim to excellence (I speak of the Greek) lies in rhythmic alertness. Particularly awkward for the commentator are lines 788-90, which in the original run, 'Think of them (i.e. Karkinos and his off-spring) as home-bred quails, neckless dancers, dwarves, snippets of sheep-shit, lovers of fancy footwork'. As every one of these descriptions needs a footnote of its own, I have replaced them with (invented) play titles. In the equivalent passage below, lines 810-11, where the original runs, 'They're both dainty-eating gorgons, skate-watching harpies, shameful old-maid-scarers, smelly-armpit fish-annihilators', I have done the same, preferring to invent play titles for Morsimos and his brother rather than the extraordinary lifestyle (making gourmet-raids on the fish-market, scattering the old maids) wished on them by most commentators and translators.

25. The presentation of Holiday was originally made to the members of the council of Athens, who sat in seats of honour at the front of the auditorium.

26. Shortened slightly from the original, which is a sequence of topical puns whose point is hard to recapture. The Greek runs: '*Trygaios:* What would you suggest? A fat bull? *Slave:* Not a bull. We don't need bullies now. *Trygaios:* A luscious pig? *Slave:* No, no. *Trygaios:* Why not? *Slave:* We don't want to provoke Theagenes' piggishness. *Trygaios:* What, then, out of all the rest? *Slave:* A sheep. (Greek: *o-ee*). *Trygaios:* A sheep? *Slave:* Yes. *Trygaios:* That's an Ionian word. *Slave:* Well, of course. If anyone in the Assembly says we must go to war, they can all sit there terrified, and say in Ionian, "Oh! Ee! Oh! Ee!". *Trygaios:* Very good. *Slave:* They'd be daft enough, too. (Greek: *OH-sin EE-pi-ee*.) Also, we'd all be more sheepish and gentle to each other and to our allies. *Trygaios:* All right, you go in and fetch a sheep. I'll get an altar to sacrifice on.'

Lysistrata

27. In the original, all the Spartans speak dialect.

28. Some scholars say that the following scene was played on two stage levels: Kinesias on the stage, Lysistrata and the women on the roof of the stage building (which represented the Akropolis battlements). Myrrhine tripped up and down between the two.

29. – either at the door, or on the upper level.

30. Herms were statues of Hermes, with erect phalluses, placed outside people's doors for luck. In 415BC, shortly before the Athenian expedition to Sicily, all the Herms in Athens were mysteriously mutilated. It became one of the most notorious political scandals of the century, and Alkibiades' supporters were blamed – not least after the expedition (on which he was one of the generals) was a disaster.

31. The story of Pylos is outlined in the introduction to *Knights*, pages xxiv–xv.

32. Karystos was famous for exporting cement.

33. The play ends with songs and dancing, in Spartan and Athenian styles. Some scholars suggest that the Chorus now represents the two sides; others that the songs were performed by soloists (the Ambassador; the Commissioner), while others danced, or by the Chorus, while soloists danced. I have remained neutral, merely indicating 'Spartan' or 'Athenian' as required.

34. Scholars suspect that some text is missing here. For artistic symmetry, the Spartan song just ended should be balanced by an Athenian song. If so, the lines are lost without trace. A second problem is that Lysistrata should surely appear at the consummation of her own triumph; but there is no indication of her entry here, as there is everywhere else in the play. Some scholars give the lines which follow to the Chorus Leader. Others imagine that Lysistrata speaks them, after appearing

here in apotheosis as the goddess Artemis, or as Athene (appropriate for her own temple, the Parthenon). I have resisted trying to resolve any of this confusion, merely suggesting that Lysistrata, not the Chorus, might speak here.

These translations follow the old Oxford Classical Text of Hall and Geldart, or new editions of individual plays currently being published by OUP, or both. All divergent readings and reallocations of characters are my own. I should like to recommend three books: K.J. Dover, *Aristophanic Comedy* (a general study, good on politics), C.H. Whitman, *Aristophanes and the Comic Hero* (interesting literary criticism), and Jeffery Henderson, *The Maculate Muse* (fascinating, not to say mind-boggling, on bawdy). My own book *The Theatre of Aristophanes* discusses Aristophanes as a practical playwright, going further into many of the issues raised in the Introductions and Notes to these translations.

WHO'S WHO

Most names are transliterated from the Greek, but when an anglicised form is more familiar – as with Aeschylus – this has been retained.

Stressed syllable is in capitals. 'ai' sounds as the 'i' in 'ice'; 'ch' as in Scots 'loch'. * before a name means that that person has his or her own entry in this list.

ADONIS (a-DOH-niss). Beautiful mortal beloved by *Aphrodite. He was killed by his own hunting hounds, and Aphrodite mourned him. 'The Adonis-song' became a standard mourning-ode in Greek poetry.

AESCHYLUS–AISCHYLOS (EESS-chil-oss or ESS-chil-oss). Real poet, quoted by Aristophanes' older characters, as typical of all that was fine about the good old days. Mocked by Aristophanes' younger characters as a wordy bore.

AESOP–AISOPOS (EE-sop). Legendary figure credited with collecting the folk-tales and anecdotes known as 'Aesop's Fables'. Aristophanes' older characters quote him as if he is some kind of fount of universal wisdom.

AGORAKRITOS (ag-o-RA-kri-toss, 'choice of the market-place'). Sausage-seller, hero of *Knights*.

AISCHINADES (essch-in-AH-dees). Invented farmer.

AMPHITHEOS (am-FI-thay-oss, 'all-round deity'). Invented god.

ANTIMACHOS (an-TI-ma-choss). Real person, one of Aristophanes' first backers. Mocked as a splutterer – which some scholars claim implies a vile but unspecified perversion involving Chorus-boys.

APHRODITE (af-ro-DIE-tee). Goddess of sexual attraction.

APOLLO–APOLLON (a-POL-loh). God of music, healing and prophecy (especially at his chief shrine at Delphi).

ARCHEPTOLEMOS (ar-chep-TOL-e-moss). Real politician.

ARIGNOTOS (ar-ig-NOH-toss). Real lyre-player, brother of *Ariphrades.

ARIPHRADES (ar-i-FRAH-dees). Real flautist, mocked by Aristophanes for liking cunnilingus.

ARTEMIS (AR-te-miss). Virgin goddess of hunting, child-birth and young creatures.

ATHENE (ath-EE-nee). Goddess of wisdom; patron of Athens. The owl was her sacred bird, on Athens' coins.

ATREUS (A-tryoos or a-TRYOOS). In myth, father of Agamemnon and Menelaus.

BACCHOS–BAKCHOS (BAK-choss). *Dionysos in his orgiastic aspect.

BAKIS (BAK-iss). Real soothsayer, but treated by Aristophanes as pedlar of fraudulent gibberish.

BRASIDAS (BRASS-i-dass). Real Spartan general.

CASTOR AND POLLUX. Twins, gods of Sparta. The Greek form of Pollux' name is Polydeukes (pol-i-DEW-kees).

CHAIRIS (CHAI-riss). Real flute-player, possibly a member of Aristophanes' company. Appears on-stage in unlikely costumes (e.g. as a nightingale in *Birds*), and is mercilessly mocked, rather as the 'band' is mocked by present-day comedians.

DEMOS (DEE-moss). Personification of the people of Athens, akin to John Bull in the UK, Uncle Sam in the USA. A fat, grumpy old man.

DEMOSTHENES (deh-moss-THEH-nees). Not the famous orator, but a general, colleague of *Nikias.

DEMOSTRATOS (dem-O-strat-oss). Real (?) politician.

DIKAIOPOLIS (dik-ai-O-po-liss, 'just city'). Hero of *Acharnians*.

DIONYSOS (die-on-EYE-soss or dee-on-i-SOSS). God of ecstasy, intoxication, artistic inspiration and drama.

ERECHTHEUS (e-rech-THYOOSS). Legendary king of Athens.

EURIPIDES (yoo-RIP-i-dees or yoo-ri-PEE-dees). Real tragedian, mocked for atheism, trendy style, hostility to women, and because his mother kept a greengrocery stall.

GANYMEDE (GAN-i-meed or gan-i-MEE-dees). In myth, a beautiful mortal youth taken by the gods to Olympos to be their cup-bearer.

GORGON. In myth, a monster whose glance turned mortals to stone. *Perseus killed it and cut off its head. The gorgon's head was often painted on shields.

GRYTTOS (GRUT-toss). Nothing known.

HERAKLES (he-RA-klees). In myth, the son of *Zeus and the mortal Alkmene. Famous in Aristophanes as a gluttonous he-man.

HERMES (HER-mees). God who led dead souls to the Underworld; messenger god; doorkeeper; patron of thieves and tricksters. Aristophanes makes him an effeminate glutton.

HIEROKLES (heer-o-KLEES, 'sacred-snatcher'). Imaginary prophet of *Bakis.

HIPPIAS (HIP-pi-ass). Tyrant of Athens, 527-510BC, forced into exile after a Spartan invasion. Sided with the Persians at the battle of Marathon.

HOMER (Greek: ho-MEER-oss). Real poet, whose *Iliad* and *Odyssey* were regarded in Athens with as much awe as the Bible in Puritan England or the Ramayana in Hindu India.

HYLAS (HI-lass). Slave name.

HYMEN (hi-MEHN). God of marriage.

HYPERBOLOS (hi-PER-bo-loss). Real lamp-maker and politician.

INO (EE-noh). In myth, the sister of *Semele, mother of *Dionysos. She brought up the child, and was punished by *Hera, queen of the gods, who drove her mad.

ION (ee-OHN). Real poet.

ISMENIAS (is-men-EE-ass, 'cleverdick'). Slave's name.

KALONIKE (ka-lo-NEE-kee, 'fine victory'). Character in *Lysistrata*.

KARKINOS (kar-KEE-nos, 'crab'). Real dancer.

KERBEROS (Greek: KER-be-ross). In myth, the guard-dog of the underworld. One of *Herakles' labours was to go to the underworld and bring Kerberos back alive.

KELEOS (ke-LAY-oss). Legendary Athenian hero.

KEPHISODEMOS (ke-fee-SO-dee-moss). Real lawyer, nick-named 'The Scythian Desert' because of his wildness and savagery.

KEPHISOPHON (ke-fee-so-FOHN). Real assistant of *Euripides. Aristophanes mocks his tragic pretensions, but also uses him because his name means 'river-babble'.

KINESIAS (kin-e-SEE-ass). (1) Real poet mocked for his *avant-garde* style. His lines are (in Greek) a mixture of his own (real) phrases and Aristophanes' parodies, and (in this English) a mixture of everyone from Keats to Hopkins, McLeish to Shakespeare. (2) Randy husband of *Myrrhine in *Lysistrata*. (Kinesias means 'Getting it up'.)

KLEISTHENES (klays-THAY-nees). A favourite butt of Athenian comedians. Camp, effeminate and pretentious: when he speaks, it is almost always in lines parodied from tragedy. No one knows if he existed in real life.

KLEOMENES (kle-o-MAY-nees). Real Spartan king, who tried to set up a puppet government in Athens but was driven out after a popular uprising.

KLEON (KLEE-on or klee-OHN). Real tanner who went into politics and was the most powerful man in Athens from 427BC until he was killed in battle. Nicknamed 'Dog' because of his yapping, snarling oratory. Virulently mocked by Aristophanes – and prone to retaliate with lawsuits.

KLEONYMOS (klee-OH-ni-moss). One of Aristophanes' favourite joke figures, mentioned over thirty times in the extant plays as a fat, greedy coward, who in the course of some battle threw away his shield and ran for safety. The battle may have been the real battle of Delion; Kleonymos may have been a real person; no one knows.

KOMARCHIDES (ko-mar-CHEE-dees). Invented farmer.

KRATES (KRAH-tees). Real actor and comic playwright.

KRATINOS (kra-TEE-noss). (1) Real comic poet, mocked by Aristophanes (but with some affection) for being past it and over-fond of drink. (2) Real but obscure lyric poet, mocked for his ridiculous haircut and his foul smell.

LAMACHOS (LA-ma-choss). Real general, who fought bravely in the war against Sparta but who is mocked by Aristophanes as a bone-headed warmonger. Perhaps his name is the reason: it means, 'too much fighting'.

LAMPITO (lam-pi-TOH). Leader of the Spartan women in *Lysistrata*. Lampito was a traditional aristocratic name in Sparta. To Athenians, it would also be connected with the verb 'to gleam', and refer to Lampito's glowing health and beauty (a quality for which Spartan women were renowned).

LYSISTRATA (lie-SISS-tra-ta, more correctly liss-iss-TRAH-tah, 'disbander of armies'). Leading character in *Lysistrata*: a lady of rank, it seems, a general's wife.

MAGNES (MAG-nees). Real comic poet.

MELANION (me-la-NEE-on). In myth, a notorious misanthrope.

MELANTHIOS (mel-anth-EE-os). Real poet and glutton.

MORSIMOS (MOR-si-moss). Real dramatist.

MYRRHINE (mir-REE-nee, 'myrtle-bough'). Flirtatious character in *Lysistrata*. Myrtle, in comedy, is always associated with sexual intercourse, perhaps (scholars say) because of its seductive perfume.

NIKARCHOS (NEE-kar-choss). Real informer.

NIKIAS (ni-KEE-ass). Real general.

OINEUS (OI-nyoos). In myth, king of Calydon who invited a party of heroes to kill a gigantic boar.

PAPHLAGON (paf-la-GOHN, 'the Paphlagonian'). Blustering main character in *Knights*. 'Paphlagon' is a slave-name (slaves were often called after the region they came from); but it also puns with *paphlazon*, 'splutterer', one of *Kleon's nicknames.

PEGASOS (PEG-a-soss). In myth, a winged horse which sprang from the blood of the *gorgon killed by *Perseus.

PEISANDROS (pay-SAN-dross). Real fat coward.

PERIKLEIDES (per-i-KLAY-dees). Real person; nothing else known.

PERIKLES (per-i-KLEES). Leading citizen of Athens during its great period of reconstruction after the Persian Wars. Nicknamed 'The Olympian' and 'The Thunderer' – names otherwise reserved for *Zeus.

PHAIAX (FIE-ax). Real orator and politician, known for making speeches which were impressive but impossible to follow.

PHAINARETE (fie-na-REE-tee, 'clearly virtuous'). According to *Amphitheos in *Acharnians*, his mother.

PHEIDIAS (FIE-dee-ass or fe-DEE-ass). Real architect and sculptor, designer of the Parthenon and the huge statue of *Athene which it contained. Sued for embezzlement soon after the work was complete.

PHILOKTETES (fil-ok-TEE-tees). In myth, he was given the magic bow of *Herakles, then banished by the gods to a desert island, whence he had to be rescued before the bow could bring about the fall of Troy.

PHOENIX–PHOINIX (FEE-nix). (1) In myth, one of the Greek heroes who fought at Troy. (2) In myth, ancestor of the Phoenician race. (3) In myth, a bird which reincarnated itself by rising from its own funeral pyre.

POSEIDON (poss-i-DOHN or poss-AI-don). *Zeus' brother, god of the sea and one of the most senior Olympian gods.

PSEUDARTABAS (psyood-ar-TA-bass). (Invented) Persian prince in *Acharnians*. His name means 'sham Artabas'; '-abas' is a royal ending in real Persian names.

SIMAITHA (sim-AI-tha). (Real?) brothel-keeper.

SITALKES (sit-AL-kees). Ruler of the Thracians (northern tribe) during the war between Athens and Sparta; loyalty to Athens in some doubt.

SOPHOCLES–SOPHOKLES (SOF-o-klees or sof-o-KLEES). Real poet, always spoken of with affection by Aristophanes.

STRATON (STRAT-ohn). (Real?) effeminate; *Kleisthenes' sidekick.

STRATONIKE (strat-o-NEE-kee, 'wins in battle'). Character in *Festival Time*.

TELEPHOS (TEH-le-foss). Hero of (lost) tragedy by *Euripides. In myth, a Mysian king wounded by Achilles en route to the Trojan War. (See Note 3 on page 257).

THEAGENES (thee-a-GAY-nees). Real boaster.

THEMISTOKLES (them-iss-to-KLEES). Real war-leader, who worked out the strategy which defeated the Persians at Salamis; later banished by his ungrateful fellow-citizens.

THEOGNIS (THEE-og-niss). Real tragic poet, mocked for his frigid style. Nickname was 'Snow'.

THOUKYDIDES (thoo-koo-DEE-dees). Not the famous historian, but an aged politician.

THOUMANTIS (THOO-man-tiss). (Real?) beggar.

TIMON (ti-MOHN). In myth, a generous man reduced to beggary by ungrateful friends, who became the very emblem of misanthropy.

TRIPTOLEMOS (trip-TO-le-moss). In myth, the inventor of ploughing. Claimed as an ancestor by *Amphitheos in *Acharnians*, rather as a Bible-educated fraud might claim to be descended from Methuselah or Noah.

TRYGAIOS (tri-GAI-oss, 'harvester'). Farmer-hero of *Peace*.

XANTHIAS (ksan-THEE-ass, 'redhead'). Slave-name.